ENDORSEMENTS

Michelle and Jenn have tackled a subject matter much needed today. Thank you for being real. Thank you for pointing women to the true source and giver of beauty. The words on these pages filled my heart with joy, inspired me to look at others instead of myself, and challenged me to a deeper call to serve. When I was little, my grandma said "pretty is as pretty does" and we learned our kind actions make us pretty.

—**Chrys Howard**, radio host and author of *Rockstar Grandparent*, co-author of *Strong and Kind* with daughter, Korie Robertson, star of *Duck Dynasty*

Jenn and Michelle's *Divine Beauty* beautifully reflects my deep heart-cry that women and girls see themselves as God sees them—made in his image, loved, and valuable. Let these truths transform and enable you to step out to become the beautiful woman of faith he created you to be! You'll be encouraged!

—**Nancy Stafford**, actress, speaker, and author of *Beauty by the Book: Seeing Yourself as God Sees You*

Michelle and Jenn have created a much-needed devotional to help focus our hearts and minds on the truth about our beauty. In a world that demands we keep up with others' standards so we'll feel worthy and valued, *Divine Beauty* takes us to the only opinion that matters: God's. Focused on Scripture's definition of what it means to be a daughter of the King, this book will become a cherished resource for women of all ages.

—**Mary Bernard**, Jesus Calling Podcast social media team, writer and editor

If only each of us could truly comprehend, believe, and absorb how much God loves and adores us—how beautiful we are to him—how much worth we have in his eyes! How would *knowing* that change every decision we make? We are bombarded with images and ideas of what it means to be worth something in this world: the perfect body, an on-trend wardrobe, the right friends, the correct political views, on-point social media with as many followers as possible, the list goes on because the enemy knows how to keep our focus anywhere but on our heavenly Father. He knows how powerful we are when we are living in his love and truth. That is why this devotional is so important, especially for young women. Beginning the day with what God says about our worth will change the trajectory of that day, and eventually our life. Pair that with the opportunity to *wear* his Word on the bracelet for a constant reminder, and we are arming our young women with a power that no one can take away!

—**Terri Conn**, Emmy-nominated actress and QVC TV host

Divine Beauty provides a great reminder of who we should strive to be as Christian women—more beautiful on the inside than out. The reflective questions help us to reevaluate our self-image through God's eyes, not through our own, which is a much more accurate perspective!

—**Lisa Burkhardt Worley**, award-winning author and radio show host

This is the most important step in your beauty and self-care process. Discovering who God made you to be and where your irresistible beauty comes from changes everything. *Divine Beauty* takes you on a journey that illuminates who you are from the inside out. The result is true peace, unspeakable joy, a radiant you, and the grace to handle whatever life brings your way. This is a must-read that is long over-due!

—**Fanchon Stinger**, TV news anchor

A valuable tool in today's world. A reminder of a woman's worth using truth and helping each live a beautifully designed life.

—**Cindy Montgomery**, national designer, New York, New York creator and designer of Belle's custom apartment furniture and couture line for *The Farmer and the Belle*

Divine Beauty has richly blessed me and my daughters as we work through knowing and believing who we are in God. Through the study of Scripture, journaling, and practical application as set forth in *Divine Beauty*, we are embracing the essence of *true* beauty based on God's truth and love.

—**Melissa M. Brunner, Esq.** executive producer, *The Farmer and The Belle*

This is a beautiful book that will encourage women—young and old— to realize how beautiful they are. God says love others as you love yourself. Jenn and Michelle's journey to help you love yourself will inspire and encourage you to be all God created you to be, bringing you to a realization of how magnificent you really are.

—**Chris Luppo**, TV producer

We're living in an age where Botox, fillers, and plastic surgery are now given as birthday gifts to teenage girls, often by their parents! The latest dream job for girls is to become influencers, basically known for being super cute on the Internet. The thing that's missing in their unending quest for the perfect hair, skin, and body is the fact that true beauty comes from within. So, the absolute must-have for everyone's makeup table is the new devotional by Michelle Cox and Jenn Gotzon Chandler, *Divine Beauty: Becoming Beautiful based on God's Truth*. *Divine Beauty* is filled with daily reminders based on Scripture, telling all of us that if you really want to be beautiful, girl, you'd better start looking inward—and upward.

—**Ann-Marie Murrell**, CEO/ publisher/author and co-author of *PolitiChicks: A Clarion Call to Political Activism* and *What Women (Really) Want*

Divine Beauty is a must-read gift for every girl and woman of faith. Because the enemy wants us to feel less-than and ugly, he hits us in the soft spot of our appearance. If a book can be LOL funny, deep-down inspiring, and filled with God's wisdom— all at the same time—*Divine Beauty* is it. Kudos to Michelle Cox and Jenn Gotzon Chandler, both role models with real hearts and impeccable credentials. (Keep this book on the bathroom counter right by your mirror!)

—**Carey Lewis**, founder of Actors, Models & Talent for Christ

This mother-daughter book works through the hard lies both young and older women face in a society focused on glamour and popularity by exploring *biblical* beauty. *Divine Beauty* and the #Beauty Bracelet™ provide the tools to find self-esteem based on God's truth.

—**Sam Sorbo**, actress, education advocate, radio host, author of *They're YOUR Kids: An Inspirational Journey for Self-Doubter to Home School Advocate*, filmed *Let There Be Light,* SamSorbo.com

If you're looking to edify your mind and body through morning devotions, *Divine Beauty* is a tool to help you look in the mirror with affection. Knowing Jenn for years, I can say she lights up the room the moment she walks in. We both work in TV and film, so we are often at the same events. When I mention her name, I usually follow it up with, she's the beautiful blonde who radiates goodness and light. And people know who I'm talking about! I love her heart, and I know you will love her too.

—**Erin Mae Miller**, TV and film producer

Divine Beauty is full of incredible wisdom, life changing stories, and biblical truths that will transform the way women of all ages think of beauty. Each chapter shines with so much inspiration and spiritual affirmations women will never look at themselves in the mirror the same way again! I highly recommend *Divine Beauty* to be a guide on how you view your self-worth. It also has a special beauty bracelet that was designed around this devotional that you will cherish forever.

—**Shannen Fields**,
award-winning actress, producer, and inspirational speaker

The master deceiver is continually trying to convince us to look into the distorted mirror of this culture and be concerned with what others think so we'll forget who and what our Creator has made us to truly be. We need this book! I enjoyed reading and discussing these devotions with my three daughters. It was a precious and powerful guide of practical insight and biblical wisdom that helped clear our vision by pointing us to the King to find the true beauty that begins within.

—**Beckah Shae**
co-founder of Shae Shoc Records, award-winning international singer, songwriter

At a time when people can be obsessed with appearances, Michelle Cox and Jenn Gotzon Chandler use real world experiences to show the vital truth that real beauty comes from within. They provide step-by-step exercises to help all women appreciate the person God meant them to be.

—**Carla Baranauckas**,
former editor for *HuffPost*, *Gannett* and *The New York Times*

Divine Beauty speaks directly about the hearts of these two authors and their love for Christ and women. This delightful well-crafted book is a true expression of God's love for his daughters, reminding us that we are created in his image, *divinely* appointed to walk in our one- of-a-kind beauty. This book and the lovely charm bracelet will help women of all ages to identify with how the Lord sees them, giving them the tools and the trinkets to share with others.

—**Shari Rigby**, actress of *Overcomer*, director, writer of *Beautifully Flawed* and motivational speaker

Divine Beauty

A 30 DAY DEVOTIONAL

BECOMING BEAUTIFUL
BASED ON GOD'S TRUTH

MICHELLE COX
JENN GOTZON

Divine Beauty
© 2019 by The Farmer and The Belle

978-1-7334694-3-2

Design by Chris Garborg | garborgdesign.com
Editorial services by Michelle Winger | literallyprecise.com

Printed in the United States of America.

21   22   23   24   25   26   27   7   6   5   4   3   2   1

CONTENTS

THE FARMER AND
THE BELLE BRAND

The Farmer and The Belle brand provides emotional security to experience true beauty and real love based on biblical and psychological principles. We provide a pathway to help you soar into the beautiful person you were created to be: divinely beautiful. Our products (movies, jewelry, devotional books, children's storybooks, and music) will impact lives, helping all ages to value themselves no matter their circumstances.

Our movie, *The Farmer and The Belle: Saving Santaland* is a hilarious Christmas romantic comedy created with family at the heart. When a NYC model spends the holidays in a small town, she falls in love with her childhood pen pal—a pig farmer—and helps save his hometown's Santaland, learning true beauty comes from the heart not just a pretty face.

Our *#Beauty Bracelet*™ is designed with a beautiful chain that holds five charms (with twenty inscriptions) that affirm the mind, body, and soul on what God defines as true beauty. The fifth charm is a heart that adjusts to fall into the palm of your hand. That charm reads "Open My Heart" with the passage to real love when you meditate on "Dear Jesus, help me grasp how wide, long, high, and deep is your love for me."

The *Divine Beauty* book by Michelle Cox and Jenn Gotzon Chandler will provide a spa for the soul experience to lead you to true beauty based on God's truth. *Divine Beauty: Becoming Beautiful based on God's Truth* focuses on the inscriptions engraved on the #Beauty Bracelet™, equipping women of all ages to see themselves as God sees them, and to then go out to serve him as beautiful models of his love.

Beautiful Mable is a children's storybook by *VeggieTales* co-creator Mike Nawrocki with illustrations by Sara Jo Floyd @ Bryartonfarm blog. The story follows Mable who does not have the 3 P's. She's not pretty, plump, or productive, but what she does have is a kind heart and she teaches the chicks at Hen Haus what truly is beautiful.

Learn more about our products (and order yours) at www.TheFarmerandTheBelle.net.

This *Divine Beauty* devotional book is great for small group study, for mothers and daughters, grandmothers and granddaughters, or girlfriends to do together.

This book is dedicated in loving memory of Jacque Sexton who taught me what it looks like to be a beautiful woman of God. And to my sweet granddaughters, Anna, Ava, and Eden. Grandmama hopes you'll always chase after Jesus.
—MICHELLE COX

I'd like to dedicate this to my precious mom, Jo-Ann Gotzon, who taught me what kindness is and how to have a beautiful heart.
—JENN GOTZON CHANDLER

Charm is deceitful and beauty is vain, But a woman who fears the LORD, she shall be praised.
PROVERBS 31:30

Hello,
BEAUTIFUL!

When Michelle starts a new book project, she often does several posts on social media to feel out her audience. She posted a question for another book project and asked, "What's in your jewelry box?" She had hundreds of quick replies with many of the responders going into great detail, and some men even popped on and told what was in their wives' jewelry boxes.

Contrast that to when she posted a question for this book asking women to tell her what they thought was beautiful about themselves. The response was eye-opening. Silence. Crickets chirping. No comments on her Facebook page. Not one. She did get a few private replies, but that was it.

She was floored. It was so unexpected. Then as she thought about it more, she realized that way too often women are their own worst enemies. They compare themselves to others and are found lacking. When they look in the mirror, get on a scale, page through a magazine with gorgeous models, or enter a crowded room, most hear or believe something negative about themselves.

The God who created us made us in his image—and he doesn't make junk.

It's time for us to quit looking at ourselves through *our* eyes and start seeing ourselves as God does. We can begin the process by transforming our thoughts and affirming our souls with biblical truths about beauty. We start to hold the lies that we're ugly or worthless to God's light and replace them with what he says about us.

This is part of the reason Jenn was burdened to create the #TrueBeauty bracelet with affirmations about what God says about women and beauty. The devotions in this book will follow the affirmations and verses featured on each charm, giving each of us a one-on-one appointment with the best beauty consultant ever—God—as he shares his tips for becoming truly beautiful.

Our *Divine Beauty* book will provide a pathway to experience beauty based on God's truth. Spend a day, a week, or a season reflecting and replacing the lies you hear, believe, or think about yourself.

Are you ready to dip into God's beauty kit, beautiful friends? Let's go!

Hugs,

Michelle and Jenn

I AM A
MAGNIFICENT MASTERPIECE

"The LORD does not see as man sees; for man looks at the outward appearance, but the LORD looks at the heart."

1 SAMUEL 16:7 NKJV

I am valuable.

I am magnificent.

I am a masterpiece.

I am beautiful.

I am made by God.

The Lord looks at my heart.

Body and soul,
I am marvelously made.

I will praise You, for I am fearfully and wonderfully made; Marvelous are Your works, and that my soul knows very well.

PSALM 139:14 NKJV

Chapter One

TRULY VALUABLE

Indeed, the very hairs of your head are all numbered.
Do not fear; you are more valuable
than many sparrows.
LUKE 12:7

FROM THE BEAUTY KIT

The word *valuable* means something of exceptional worth.
It's something that is often set apart from the ordinary.

We girls love our accessories, don't we? Whether it's a designer handbag, cute shoes, or jewelry bling, it often makes us feel prettier and completes our look. I sometimes joke that my handbag and my jewelry are my diet plan. Maybe people won't notice my extra pounds if they're focused on my accessories.

A while back I was in a dinner club group with some sweet friends whose bank statements had way more zeroes than mine. Their lives were filled with exotic trips, and their social lists included well-known influential people whose names you'd recognize. I'm still not quite sure how they ended up with me, but I'm glad they did. Our group gathered each month at a different restaurant, and we had so much fun together.

When we met for dinner one night, I wore the jewelry—a ring, bracelet, and earrings—that my husband had bought me for Christmas. One of my friends gasped when she saw them, "Black sapphires! Do you know how rare they are? Your husband did g*ood* for you this Christmas." All of them gushed about my jewelry.

I sat there chuckling on the inside. You see, I knew something they didn't. I'd picked the jewelry out so I knew they were just high-quality costume jewelry. My husband had paid several hundred dollars for them, but they weren't real stones. My wedding rings and some other pieces are real jewels, but I discovered years ago that people usually can't tell the difference between real and fake jewelry, so why spend the extra money when only a jeweler would recognize the difference?

Many of us look at our lives and think we're junk: that there's no real value to us. But God thinks differently. He says, "You are valuable." Jesus loves you so much that he willingly gave his *life* for you. How could you possibly be more valuable to someone than that?

Isaiah 43:1 says, "I have called you by name; you are Mine!" It blows me away that the God who made the universe knows my name. Matthew 10:30 tells us that he cares so much about us that he numbers the hairs on our heads. Isaiah 49:16 says, "Behold, I have inscribed you on the palms of My hands." Did you catch that? Every time God clasps his hands together, you are right there, held between his hands.

In Isaiah 43:4, he tells us, "You are precious in My sight." And

> Jesus loves you so much that he willingly gave his life for you.
>
> How could you possibly be more valuable to someone than that?

in Jeremiah 31:3, God says, "I have loved you with an everlasting love."

Sweet friend, wrap this truth around you like a warm sweater on a cold day. Say these words out loud, "I am valuable because God says I am." Feel the warmth of his peace and comfort and the blessing of his love. Then walk with confidence because you are his valued and beloved child.

Father, sometimes I feel like I'm not worth anything at all, but you say I'm valuable. That humbles and amazes me. Help me to remember that my worth is found in you. Remind me that the more I live like you, the more valuable I'll become. I want to share your message of hope to others who need to know that they are valuable. Help me guard my tongue so my words will always uplift others instead of cutting them down or leaving scars on their hearts. Thank you for loving me so much. Amen.

BEAUTY QUESTIONNAIRE

1. Why is it important for you to tell others that they're valuable to you and to God?
2. What are three spiritual traits that you already have? What three spiritual traits would you like to instill in your life?
3. How does it make you feel to know that God knows the number of hairs on your head and that he has engraved your name on the palms of his hands?

GET YOUR STILETTOS MOVING

Re-read all the Scriptures in the devotion. Everywhere you see the word "you," use your name instead. Ask God to place two friends on your heart who need to hear this message. Let them know they're valuable to you and to God.

THE MIRROR OF YOUR HEART

How does it affect the mirror
of your heart to know that
God says you are valuable?

_____

_____

_____

_____

_____

_____

Chapter Two

A MAGNIFICENT HEART

God created man in His own image; in the image of God He created him; male and female He created them.
GENESIS 1:27 NKJV

FROM THE BEAUTY KIT

The word *magnificent* means something that's impressive, notable, or superb beyond the norm. It stands out from the rest and people notice.

My granddaughters—ages six, seven, and nine—love playing with makeup. My daughter-in-law bought them small makeup kits so they could play with them (and stay out of their mother's makeup).

My six-year-old granddaughter, Eden, is a pro at eye makeup. Seriously. I've asked her to do my eyes and show me how she does it. She's that good. But lipstick? That's another story.

A friend from church shared that Eden recently came bopping into her Sunday school class with a big smile and bright purple lipstick that looked like she'd gone around her lips four or five times. Her teeth also sported purple lipstick.

Eden's mom was taken aback when she saw her daughter later that morning. When they'd left for church, Lydia hadn't seen her. Eden had run out first and hopped into her car seat in the back of their big SUV. She jumped out quickly when they arrived at church and zipped to her Sunday school class.

Miss Eden felt magnificent that morning. But if she is like most females, as she gets older, her image of herself will change. She might believe the lies Satan whispers to her or the words that others say. She may compare herself to the images in magazines or online and will find herself lacking.

Sweet friend, today is the day to stomp on those lies, to imagine yourself as the magnificent person God created. Say the words out loud, "I am magnificent. (Insert your name) is magnificent."

Any bit of physical beauty was made by God and when we strive to be more like him, that outward beauty is enhanced because of the loveliness of our hearts. Beauty of heart and soul is something we have to work at because we start with hearts that are filled with sin. This is where our choices come into play each day. We must choose forgiveness instead of bitterness. We must grant kindness instead of what's deserved. And we must give love when it isn't warranted.

I recently quizzed my Facebook friends about things they thought were magnificent. I received lots of answers, and here's the thing that really struck me: they didn't mention works of

> Magnificence is the unspeakable and indescribable joy that wells deep inside of me as deep calls to deep—the song the Holy Spirit sings when my soul recognizes my God's presence.
>
> —KAREN SHAFER

art, bestselling books, or famous music. They talked about God's creation. A newborn baby. Answers to prayer. Family.

What *could* be more magnificent than a newborn baby or a vivid sunset? There's only one thing I can think of, and that's a woman whose life is completely sold out to God. That's where we'll discover true magnificent beauty that others can't help but notice.

As my friend Karen Shafer says, "Magnificence cannot be captured in a photo or an object. It's the unspeakable and indescribable joy that wells deep inside of me as deep calls to deep—the song the Holy Spirit sings when my soul recognizes my God's presence." Now *that* is magnificent.

Father, so many times I look at myself and see a loser. I focus on my flaws. Others don't have to tear me down because I'm so good at doing it myself. And yet, you have made me magnificent. I'm made in your likeness, so how could I help but be that way? Renew my mind with this knowledge. Let it sink in to the deepest parts of my heart and soul and help me to grasp it as I never have before. Help me to apply this magnificence to my life as if I'm putting on makeup— enhancing the beauty you've given me, so I can glorify you. Amen.

BEAUTY QUESTIONNAIRE

1. Why is it important for you to realize that God designed you to be magnificent?
2. Why should you want to be magnificent for him?
3. What are some traits that will make your soul magnificent?

GET YOUR STILETTOS MOVING

It's easy to be average, but it takes consistent work to become exceptional. Spend some extra time in God's Word and in prayer and ask him to show you three specific talents or gifts that he has given you so you can be magnificent for him. Do those things, and then thank him for creating you with those gifts.

THE MIRROR OF YOUR HEART

I AM MAGNIFICENT.

How does it affect the mirror of your heart to know that you can become magnificent for God?

_____

_____

_____

_____

_____

_____

Chapter Three

A MASTERPIECE

We are God's masterpiece. He has created us anew in Christ Jesus, so we can do the good things he planned for us long ago.
Ephesians 2:10 nlt

FROM THE BEAUTY KIT

The word *masterpiece* describes someone's greatest work, something they've done with a masterly skill and excellence that exceeds what most other people can accomplish. Masterpieces are things of exceptional beauty that can affect many generations.

God describes us as his masterpiece, but a recent stop in front of my mirror for a leisurely inspection of myself left a less than stellar impression. Age spots and wrinkles have had the nerve to settle on my face. Forget a bad hair day, I seem to be having a bad hair life. Dark circles from not enough rest have taken up permanent residence under my eyes, leaving me looking somewhat like a raccoon with smeared mascara. Let's not even discuss the pudgy face, double chin, and the turkey neck that wobbles when I talk. I imagine some of you feel the same when you look at yourself and wonder how in the world could God consider you a masterpiece.

It really does describe us, though, because God looks beyond our outward appearance to what makes us truly beautiful. He made us with hope and a purpose. He created us with wisdom to lean not on our understanding but on his. He designed us with the ability to make choices. We can choose joy, gratitude, and peace, all traits that make us lovely.

> You are beautiful because God is an artist and you are his masterpiece.

The King James version says that we are his "workmanship." God is a master craftsman and what he makes is never junk. God has given us fingers so we can touch others with his love, feet so we can go help those who need it, ears to hear others who need someone to care. All of you is a delicate masterpiece that he has designed. Believe it. *You* are God's masterpiece.

What's so wonderful about this is that—as I discovered from my time in front of the mirror—the passing of years often brings a downhill slide to our outward appearance, but our inward appearance can just keep becoming more and more beautiful as the years go by… as long as we've lived those years for Jesus.

I'm sure Leonardo da Vinci never dreamed that his painting of the Mona Lisa would become the number one art masterpiece in the world. Michelangelo spent years working to complete the fresco in the Sistine Chapel. There must have been days when he became discouraged and went home thinking he'd just painted absolute junk. There were probably even naysayers who told these artists their work was terrible. But, today, these works of art are recognized as masterpieces.

Satan excels at whispering negative thoughts to us. *You're fat. You're ugly. No one will ever love you. You'll never amount to anything.* That voice, those thoughts, those lies often torment us. We need to identify the lies, quit listening to the wrong voice, and bring the lies into the light of God's truth. He says, "*You* are my workmanship, my *masterpiece.*" If God says we are his masterpiece, who are we to dispute him?

Father, help me grasp at my core that I am your masterpiece and you've created me for your glory. The Mona Lisa and the fresco in the Sistine Chapel are masterpieces that have touched people for hundreds of years. I want to be that kind of masterpiece for you: one whose life is lived in such a manner that others will see the beauty of you. I want to be the kind of masterpiece for you that my family will talk about for generations to come as they remember that I loved you, I loved them, I prayed for them, I served others, and I lived with purpose for you. My heart's desire is that my soul will be something of exceptional beauty for you. Amen.

BEAUTY QUESTIONNAIRE

1. Why is it often so difficult to believe that you are God's masterpiece?
2. Why is it so easy to believe Satan's lies?
3. Masterpieces are often around for centuries. What do you hope to leave behind someday?

GET YOUR STILETTOS MOVING

We too often believe Satan's lies. We need to replace those lies with God's truth. It's been said that it takes twenty-one days to build a new habit. Mark your calendar with the day you start, and for the next three weeks, begin and end your day with these words, "God says I am a masterpiece."

THE MIRROR OF YOUR HEART

I AM A MASTERPIECE.

How does it affect the mirror of your heart to know that God says you are a masterpiece?

_____

_____

_____

_____

_____

_____

Chapter Four

MY FATHER SAYS SO

Your adornment must not be merely external—
braiding the hair, and wearing gold jewelry, or putting on
dresses; but let it be the hidden person of the heart, with the
imperishable quality of a gentle and quiet spirit, which is
precious in the sight of God.

1 PETER 3:3-4

FROM THE BEAUTY KIT

The word *beautiful* describes something extraordinary or incredible—something that gives others great delight to see or hear, such as a heart-stirring concert, a lovely sunset, or someone with great physical beauty.

I knew a woman (we'll call her Betty) who was beautiful. Even though she had grandchildren, her figure was still great and she loved to show off her shapely legs. She was delighted whenever anyone told her she was beautiful.

I'd learned from personal experience that she was quite vain and that she wasn't nice to people who didn't recognize her beauty or make her the center of attention.

I once asked her what they were doing now that her husband (we'll call him Bob) was retired. She said, "Oh, it's a wonderful life! We sleep in and then Bob fixes breakfast. We play cards, and then I go lay out by the pool all afternoon so I can keep my tan. When I come inside, I get fixed up and we go shopping then out to dinner." Her whole existence was about her.

She continued, "I just don't understand why the women at the pool are so catty. They barely speak to me. I guess it's because I'm so beautiful and they don't measure up."

Contrast that with my friend, Debbie, who is lovely but doesn't seem to know it. Her days are filled with serving others. People flock to her because of her beautiful spirit, laughter, and genuine concern.

As my friend Daphne Woodall says, "Beauty on the outside can't make up for ugly on the inside." But beauty on the inside far outweighs outward beauty, and inward beauty never fades.

> Beauty on the outside can't make up for ugly on the inside.
>
> —Daphne Woodall

It's often said that beauty is in the eye of the beholder. We gaze in awe at God's glorious creations, but when we look at ourselves—another of God's glorious creations—we somehow see anything but beauty.

Makeup can correct many flaws in our outward appearance, but it doesn't correct soul wounds about how we see ourselves. Many times those wounds have come from others who told us we were ugly, fat, or not good enough. Often we carry those hurtful words with us for the rest of our lives.

We look in the mirror and see nothing but pudgy faces, hairy chins, and acne scars. But all that changes when the Creator of the universe looks at us and says, "You are beautiful." God created us in his image. How could we be anything but beautiful? My little granddaughter, Ava, is truly beautiful. Even better, she has a sweet and loving spirit. People stop us all the time to comment on her beauty and her gorgeous red hair. But one day, a playmate told her she wasn't pretty. When she told me about it, I said, "What did you tell him?"

"I told him I was too beautiful because my daddy tells me that every day."

Maybe we need to follow young Ava's example and believe the words our Father whispers to our souls, "My daughter, you are beautiful."

Father, help me to accept myself and to love myself not because of anything I've done, but because you made me beautiful. Help me to listen to the words that you speak to my soul. I've often prayed for you to help me see others through your eyes, but today I ask you to let me see myself through your eyes. God, it boggles my mind that you see something beautiful when you look at me. Groom my heart to be something of exceptional loveliness for you, and as I meet people each day, let them see the beauty of you in me. Amen.

BEAUTY QUESTIONNAIRE

1. How can being vain affect you and your relationships?
2. How do soul wounds from the past affect how you see yourself today?
3. How did the daily words Ava heard from her daddy impact how she felt about herself? What can her example teach you about listening when God says that you're beautiful?

GET YOUR STILETTOS MOVING

Replace every negative lie you hear about yourself with the words "I am beautiful—because God says so." Start by making a list of the beautiful things you find about your outward appearance. (Do you have pretty eyes, a sparkling smile, or a lovely complexion?) Next, make a list of specific ways that you can become more beautiful on the inside.

THE MIRROR OF YOUR HEART

How does it affect the mirror of your heart to know that *God* says you are beautiful?

_____

_____

_____

_____

_____

_____

Chapter Five

THE MASTER DESIGNER

God created man in His own image; in the image of God He created him; male and female He created them.
GENESIS 1:27 NKJV

FROM THE BEAUTY KIT

The word *made* describes something that has been created, invented, or crafted. The word *God* describes the Creator of the universe, the one who made us.

Middle school and high school can be tough—especially for those who are insecure or have low self-esteem. There's the pressure of entering an unknown environment and 62,475 fears and worries that hit us as we do. *Will I fit in? What if they think I'm ugly? Will they think I'm a nerd? What should I wear? Are these shoes out of style? How can I hide this boulder-sized zit on my face? Should I do my hair in a ponytail, braid, or curl it? What if they don't like me?*

Peer pressure is enormous. Add in fears regarding living our faith, and it can be even scarier. *Will they think I'm weird because I'm a Christian? Will they make fun of me? Will I have the courage to put my faith on display, or will I hide it because I want to be one of the cool kids? Will I tell others about God, or will I keep the best news ever a well-kept secret?*

We were made by the King of Kings. We are his beloved daughters, and that makes us princesses.

We've all been there. We've all had those worries. Many of us never outgrow them. But here's the thing: we can walk with confidence through life and through the hallways of our schools. After all, we were made by the King of kings. We are his beloved daughters, and that makes us princesses.

He made us in his image, and that means we're beautiful because he is a beautiful and amazing God. In Jeremiah 1:4-5, he tells us, "Before I formed you in the womb I knew you, and before you were born I consecrated you; I have appointed you a prophet to the nations."

Isaiah 64:8 says, "O LORD, You are our Father, we are the clay, and You our potter; and all of us are the work of Your hand."

When master potters make a new mug or bowl, they make exactly what they want. It's the same with God. He formed us. He molded us. He set us apart so the nations could come to know him through us.

The next time those ugly worries and fears fill your head, imagine that each of them is on a chalkboard and you're erasing them one by one. Get rid of them so they don't hold you back from serving God and becoming the woman he desires you to be. Fill the chalkboard with these words instead: I am special because

God made me. I am the work of his hand. God made me exactly how he wanted me to be. I am beautiful because I'm formed in his image. My Father is the King of kings, and that makes me a princess. He has a purpose for me. Because of all that, I can walk through each day with confidence.

Father, instead of looking in the mirror and focusing on my flaws, help me to see myself through your eyes. Thank you for forming me exactly how you wanted me to be. Help me to look at myself and say, "This is how God made me, and he does all things well." As I walk through the hallways of my school, or through the corridors of life, help me to walk in your confidence. Remind me that I am a daughter of the King. Give me boldness to share my faith, to tell others about my amazing God, and to fulfill your purpose for me. Amen.

BEAUTY QUESTIONNAIRE

1. Why do you worry about what other people think?
2. How does it make a difference to know that your Father is the King of kings—and you are his princess?
3. How can you replace your fears with confidence?

GET YOUR STILETTOS MOVING

Ask God to show you one friend who is struggling with confidence and another friend who needs more courage to live out her faith. Become their encourager. Replace the lies that Satan whispers to them, and share the truths you've learned here.

THE MIRROR OF YOUR HEART

I AM MADE BY GOD.

How does it affect the mirror of your heart to know that you are made by God?

_____

_____

_____

_____

_____

_____

_____

Chapter Six

LOOKING AT THE HEART

The LORD said to Samuel, "Do not look at his appearance or at his physical stature, because I have refused him. For the LORD does not see as man sees; for man looks at the outward appearance, but the LORD looks at the heart."

1 SAMUEL 16:7 NKJV

FROM THE BEAUTY KIT

The word *look* means to gaze at something in order to see it, or to search or examine something. The word *heart* describes our inner part—our personality, feelings, and emotions.
It's the deepest part of us.

The holiday season had arrived, along with big crowds at the department store. I groaned as I saw the long line at the gift-wrap counter, but I needed boxes, and I'd bought enough that day to get a free deluxe gift wrap, so it was worth the wait.

People have always fascinated me, so I watched the customers in line. Some were patient. Some looked grumpy. And others spent their time talking to the folks waiting in line with them.

I noticed an elderly lady a couple of people ahead of me. She was probably around eighty, but she was so beautiful. Her soft-looking white hair was cut in a cute style that complimented her features. Her makeup was tasteful and flattering. And her shoes and outfit were casual but stylish.

I tapped her on the shoulder. When she turned and looked at me, I said, "You are the most beautiful lady. I've just been standing here thinking that, and I wanted you to know."

Other people commented that they'd just been thinking the same thing. She was visibly touched. "Nobody's told me that in years. Thank you so much."

> Our faces are like the road maps of our lives. They tell the story of where we've been and what we've done.

I've often thought that our faces are like the road maps of our lives. They tell the story of where we've been and what we've done. This lady's face said that she'd been sweet, had laughed a lot, and had an inner beauty that matched her outward beauty.

You know what really struck me about that moment? The way she'd lived her life with her beautiful heart had become part of her outward appearance.

Friends, the way we live each day becomes part of the stories, the road maps, of our lives. They can say we traveled closely with Jesus each day or that we traveled as far away from him as we could get.

If you're one who has walked away from God, the good news is that the road back to him is never closed. Love, forgiveness, and mercy will be waiting for you when you arrive back home.

It's always the best choice to stay as close to Jesus as we can. Where we can soak up his sweetness. Where we can learn from his example. Where we can spend time with him and hear what he wants to say.

We need to stay close enough so he can examine our hearts and see what changes need to be made there. What hard feelings we harbor that will make us bitter. What sins need to be cleansed from our lives. And even what parts of our hearts we're withholding from him.

If we'll come to God with hearts that are tender, if we'll walk with him throughout our lifetime, we'll become more and more like him, and that will be reflected in our faces. What could make us more beautiful than that? What could be more wonderful than a countenance that sparkles for Jesus?

Dear Father, when you look at my heart, I know you'll find things that shouldn't be there. That makes me sad. Give me a heart that is tender and receptive when you come to me with things that I must change if I want to be more like you. When you search my soul, I hope that you'll also find things that will touch your heart as I strive to live for you. Help me to be so in tune with you that I hear your heartbeat, that I hear your sweet whispers to my soul. Help my countenance to shine for you, and help others to see you in me. Amen.

BEAUTY QUESTIONNAIRE

1. How is your face like a road map, and how does that apply to you spiritually?
2. What will God find when he searches your heart?
3. Why is a tender heart so important in your relationship with Jesus? And how can having a heart that is beautiful for him also be reflected in your countenance?

GET YOUR STILETTOS MOVING

Think of two women who are beautiful because of how they live for God. Tell them how their hearts for him have touched you, and then ask them about the things they've learned as they've traveled through life with Jesus.

THE MIRROR OF YOUR HEART

THE LORD
LOOKS AT
THE HEART.

What does it do to the mirror of
your heart to know that God is searching there?

_____

_____

_____

_____

_____

_____

_____

Chapter Seven

WELL-KEPT SECRET

I praise you, for I am fearfully and wonderfully made.
Wonderful are your works; my soul knows it very well.
PSALM 139:14 ESV

FROM THE BEAUTY KIT

The word *body* describes our physical structure, the outward
appearance that everyone sees. The word *soul* describes the part
of us that has life and feelings and can take action. The soul is a
separate entity from the body and it controls aspects of morality
and character. It's immortal. Our daily choices affect the health
and well-being of our souls.

I am horizontally challenged. I've always loved shopping with
my friends, but hated that the curvy department always seemed to
be in a far corner of the store—drawing attention to the fact that I
wear plus-size clothes. I generally just walked through the skinny
girl departments with my girlfriends and waited to shop for my
clothes until I was alone.

One day as I passed a mirror in the mall and got a look at my larger-than-life self, it was like the mirror shouted, "It's not a well-kept secret! They *know*!"

I suspect some of you might relate to that, and I imagine many of you have been on the diet escalator with me. Up and down. Up and down. Up, up, and away! I exercise, but now that I'm an old grandma-type, I've come to the conclusion that I'll probably never be thin. Yet I can't tell you the times I've let my weight control my life, and even allowed it to keep me from doing things for God because I was ashamed of how I looked.

I obviously haven't done too well controlling the living-history-museum of food that has attached to my hips, but I can take my eyes off the negatives and start looking for the blessings I can praise God for today and for the ways that I can serve him.

God doesn't make junk, so quit treating yourself that way.

As I worship an Almighty God, I can thank him for creating me: for eyes that can see my loved ones, for fingers that can move and pick things up, for feet and legs that take me where I want to go, for ears that hear beloved voices, and for a brain that works. And I can thank him for the fact that even with my extra pounds, he still says that I am marvelously made.

Today I praise him for a soul that's a lifeline between him and me—that we're connected through God the Father, Jesus the Son, and the Holy Spirit. I thank him for a soul that gives conviction when I'm headed down a wrong path, a soul that can feel the pain of others.

I'm reminded that the soul is a divine gift, and it's only when we dig deep to pull out our soul wounds (even our obsessions with our weight) and bring them into the light for God's healing, that he can replace the lie with his truth: we are fearfully and marvelously made for the purpose of fellowshipping with him and serving him.

You know what I've discovered with the beauty of hindsight? The weight didn't matter when it came to giving love to those who needed it, telling others about our amazing God, or doing acts of service for those who needed to know somebody cared. Once I got the weight of my failures off me, my soul could soar as the beautiful creation God designed it to be.

Dear Lord, I sure am good at finding all my flaws, and then I allow Satan to use them to defeat me. I believe his lies that I'm not good enough, that I'm not well-spoken or talented, that I'm not beautiful enough. And because of that I've often taken a back seat and allowed others to do what you asked me to do. Today, Lord, I bring you my wounds of hurtful words and shattered self-esteem, and I ask you to heal me and free me so I can accomplish the tasks you've asked me to do. Remind me that you think I'm marvelously made because you made me. Help me to become a woman whose soul is beautiful for you. Amen.

BEAUTY QUESTIONNAIRE

1. What physical things control you, and how are they keeping you from serving Jesus?
2. Why do you so often believe Satan's lies instead of God's truth?
3. What are two ways your soul could soar for God?

GET YOUR STILETTOS MOVING

Take a good look at yourself and discover ways that your body and soul are marvelously made. Write those things down today and believe them. God doesn't make junk, so quit treating yourself that way.

THE MIRROR OF YOUR HEART

BODY AND SOUL,
I AM
MARVELOUSLY
MADE.

How does it affect the mirror of
your heart to know that God says both your
body and soul
are marvelously made?

_____

_____

_____

_____

_____

_____

I AM
AN OVERCOMER

Little children, you are from God and have overcome them,
for he who is in you is greater than he who is in the world.
1 JOHN 4:4 ESV

I am transformed.

I am an overcomer.

I am renewing my mind.

I will bring the lie into the light
and replace it with God's truth.

He heals the brokenhearted.

Do not be overcome by evil, but overcome evil with good.
ROMANS 12:21 NKJV

Chapter Eight

A TRANSFORMED HEART

Do not be conformed to this world, but be transformed by the renewing of your mind, that you may prove what is that good and acceptable and perfect will of God.

ROMANS 12:2 NKJV

FROM THE BEAUTY KIT

The word *transform* means to make a big or noticeable change. Transformation is a process that usually takes time and effort but the results are worth it.

I love cupcakes. I can walk into a cupcake shop and almost hear the angels singing *The Hallelujah Chorus*. One day I was certain that I even saw a beam of light from heaven spotlighting the cupcake display. My husband said it was just the glare from a car windshield outside, but what does he know?

Those soft and fluffy rounds of cake are delightful. The mile-high mounds of frosting call out, "Come to me, baby!" Somehow, I always answer. And, of course, I can't buy just one. The people who own the store have to make a living. If I don't buy a container of cupcakes, they might not be able to pay their bills. I couldn't live with the guilt of that now could I?

It seems I've passed the cupcake gene down to two of my grandchildren. I'm sure I would flunk grandparent school if I didn't buy—and share—cupcakes with them. One has to rationalize these things.

Cupcakes rank as number one on my list, but I also love chocolate, and hot bread, and, well, let me make this easy: I basically love every food that isn't good for me. Let's just say that never in my lifetime have I craved a carrot stick or waxed poetic about broccoli.

But then I realized something. Those cupcakes and all those other not-good-for-me items were causing bulges in my clothes (the nerve of them!), and higher numbers in my cholesterol, blood sugar, and blood pressure. About ten years ago, I decided that I'd need a different mindset if I was going to be healthy. I started eating more good-for-me foods, cut back on my beloved cupcakes, and started exercising regularly.

> If we want to grow into women with beautiful hearts for God, we must allow him to do his work in us and transform us into what he wants us to become.

I discovered that once my mind was transformed, changes started happening, and it didn't take long until I was healthier and feeling better about myself. The truth is that most women don't see themselves as beautiful. We need to transform our thinking from the lies of *I'm fat, ugly, and worthless* to *I'm beautiful, magnificent, and made by God.*

The same is true spiritually. We become stagnant, and no growth happens when we just stay the same. If we want to see ourselves as beautiful women of faith, to be more like Christ, it begins by renewing our minds.

We can start by identifying areas where we want God to transform us. Maybe it's unconditional love for others, or traits such as living a pure life, having joy, peace, patience, kindness, or self-control. Maybe it's to become more hospitable or to provide friendship or acts of service for others. The perfect place to start is with prayer.

Change doesn't happen overnight. It's a process, and sometimes it's a painful one. But if we want to grow into the beautiful women of faith that God sees in us, we must allow him to transform us into what he wants us to become.

Dear Jesus, transform me each day to become more and more like you. Renew my mind and help me to focus on you and how I can live more for you each day. Show me what joy, peace, patience, kindness, faithfulness, gentleness and self-control look like, and how they'll impact my life and the lives of others. I know that sometimes the changes you'll ask me to make will be difficult, and I'm so grateful that you don't expect perfection. Help me to be courageous, to overcome the lies that say I'll never amount to anything. Set my heart on you and make me a beautiful shining reflection of you to those around me. Amen.

BEAUTY QUESTIONNAIRE

1. Why is it important to transform our minds first if we want change to happen?
2. Why is spiritual change sometimes painful?
3. How does transforming our minds tie in to becoming inwardly beautiful?

GET YOUR STILETTOS MOVING

Make a list of three things you want to change physically and three things you want to change spiritually. Make a second list of the things that keep you from doing that. (It helps to be aware of the roadblocks you put up in your life.) What steps do you need to take to transform your mind so you can accomplish the things on your first list?

THE MIRROR OF YOUR HEART

I AM TRANSFORMED.

How does it affect the mirror of your heart to know that your heart and life can be transformed?

_____

_____

_____

_____

_____

_____

Chapter Nine

AN OVERCOMER

*In all these things we are more than conquerors
through him who loved us.*
ROMANS 8:37 NIV

FROM THE BEAUTY KIT

The words *overcomer* or *conqueror* describe someone who
defeats an enemy or struggle, has success over temptation
or weakness, or determines that they will conquer a situation
no matter what it takes to do so.

My friend, Missy, is beautiful. She reminds me of a Barbie
doll brought to life. Her hair always looks like she has come
straight from the salon, and her smile is worthy of a toothpaste
commercial. Her makeup looks like a professional makeup artist
has worked her magic for a red carpet event. Add a cute figure,
fashionable clothes, perfectly-accessorized jewelry, and shoes, and
she is screen-ready. Every. Single. Day. She even looks like that
when she goes fishing with her husband.

She is basically everything I am not.

My pal, Carol, is one of those gals who just sparkles. I always think of her as the bling queen because she loves jewelry and clothes that have pizazz. Her personality is larger than life, and people are drawn to her because of that.

I'll never have Carol's flair for fashion. It just isn't in me.

Oh my, we so often make comparisons, don't we? We look at other people and find ourselves lacking. We need to overcome that to realize God made us *exactly* like he wants us. We need to quit listening to Satan's lies that we're ugly, or worthless, or we'll never amount to anything.

> We can't get over our pasts and what we used to be or do. We need to quit recycling those thoughts.

What if we made comparisons about inner beauty? You see, part of what makes my friends Missy and Carol so beautiful is that they both have a fierce love for God, and they're using their talents and time to touch the lives of others. The love of Jesus is what makes both of them sparkle and shine. They inspire me. These are the kinds of comparisons we need, because as it says in Proverbs 27:17 "iron sharpens iron." We can help provide accountability to each other as we strive to live for God. Friends who are sold out to Jesus will make us want to be our best for him.

Sometimes we have trouble overcoming our lack of self-esteem or confidence. We've believed Satan's lies. We've believed the words that others have said about us, or even the things we've told ourselves. Or we can't get over our pasts and what we used to be or do. We need to quit recycling those thoughts.

Sweet friend, it's time to say the words, "I'm an overcomer!" Say them out loud. Apply those words to your soul wounds—your fears, anxieties, emotional pain, health challenges, or even your body weight. It's time to take authority over the trauma in your life. Look ahead to the future God has for you instead of being stuck in the past. Quit letting the memories haunt you.

Picture Jesus standing at the foot of the cross. He is waiting for you to bring your burdens to him, but you have to be willing to let go of them. And when you do, it will set you free to truly walk through life as an overcomer—as the beautiful woman he wants you to be.

Lord, I so often make comparisons to other people and find myself lacking. The scars of my past have clung to me for so long. The bitter words that have been hurled at me caused wounds in my heart that I've never gotten over. I'm tired of carrying all the baggage. Help me to bring all my burdens to you and leave them there. Help me to be an overcomer, to conquer the past so I can look forward to the future. Thank you for the encouragers in my life. Help me to spur my family and friends on to love you more and serve you better. Amen.

BEAUTY QUESTIONNAIRE

1. Why do you so often make comparisons to other people?
2. Who inspires you to be a better Christian? Why?
3. Why is it important for you to become an overcomer?

GET YOUR STILETTOS MOVING

Make a list of three things you need to overcome in your life whether they are emotional, physical, or spiritual. Find someone who's trying hard to live for Jesus. Ask them if they'll be your iron-sharpens-iron friend and then work together on what you want to overcome, and encourage each other along the way.

THE MIRROR OF YOUR HEART

I AM AN OVERCOMER.

How does it affect the mirror of your heart when you determine that you'll become an overcomer?

_____

_____

_____

_____

_____

_____

Chapter Ten

THE NEW YOU

Be renewed in the spirit of your mind.
EPHESIANS 4:23 NKJV

FROM THE BEAUTY KIT

When we *renew* something it means we come back to it, we start it again, or we become like new physically or spiritually. It's a time of freshening that sometimes means stepping out in faith.

Have you ever gotten in a rut with your hairstyle, makeup, or fashion? I know I have, and part of the reason for that is that I don't like change. It's easy to get stuck in a routine, isn't it? To wear the old shoes that we've worn to cozy perfection or the shirt that has such comfortable fabric. It can feel odd to change to a brighter shade of lipstick when we've worn more muted tones. And sometimes we hang on to our old clothes because we haven't had time or money to buy new ones, because we love an old sweater or jeans, or maybe even because an item of clothing has sentimental value.

But sometimes change, or a time of renewal, is necessary. That can be scary, particularly when it comes to trying out a new haircut or color. If it turns out the way we hoped, it's fabulous and makes us feel wonderful. But if that new short cut looks awful on us, or the new highlights turn our hair gray instead of blonde (as mine did one time), it seems like it takes forever before the botched results grow out or can be fixed.

It's the same with us spiritually. Sometimes we've walked away from our faith or we've distanced ourselves from God. At times, his sweet whispers to our souls are enough to bring us home to him. But at other times it requires him sending tough circumstances and difficult lessons to get through to our hard hearts. When that happens, it's not because he doesn't love us; it's because he does, and he misses the precious fellowship he had with us in the past.

> Renewing our minds often necessitates a big step of faith, and it can require us getting out of our comfort zones where we have no choice but to trust God.

Renewing our minds often necessitates a big step of faith, and it can require us getting out of our comfort zones where we have no choice but to trust God.

My daughter-in-law does hair and makeup for weddings. For bridal portraits and wedding days, women sometimes don't trust their own skills. They want someone with experience so they will look their best.

As we take the first step of faith, it's nerve-wracking, especially when we can't see the end results or we wonder how we're going to find the money or gain the skills to do what God wants us to do. But he never calls us to a task without equipping us with all that we will need, and we can always trust him.

Sometimes the answer comes through someone who is an expert or through friends who will walk the journey with us. There's power in worshipping together, praying together, or having (or being) an encourager along the way.

When a woman fulfills the calling God has placed on her heart, it's an inspiration for other women to renew their minds, to step out in faith, and to follow him. What could be more beautiful than that?

Father, I know that renewing my mind is important, but it can be scary as I venture into unknown territory like a new school or job. It's intimidating when I step out in faith. Thoughts jumble through my mind like a kaleidoscope. What if I fail? I don't know anyone. I don't know what I'm doing. But I know that you have the answers to all my concerns. Thank you for always being with me. Help me to trust you. As I come into contact with those who have wandered away from you, remind me to pray for them, that their hearts will be renewed and strengthened, and that they will return to you. Amen.

BEAUTY QUESTIONNAIRE

1. Why is change, or a time of renewal, sometimes so scary?
2. When God sends tough circumstances to you to get your attention, how does that show his love for you?
3. When you step out in faith, why is it important for you to have a Christian friend to walk the journey with you?

GET YOUR STILETTOS MOVING

Spend some time with God today. Ask him to show you areas in your life where you need to be renewed, and then set some specific goals to get started on that.

THE MIRROR OF YOUR HEART

How does it affect the mirror of
your heart when you go through
a time of renewal with God?

_____

_____

_____

_____

_____

_____

_____

Chapter Eleven

THE WRONG THING

"I do not pray that You should take them out of the world, but that You should keep them from the evil one. Sanctify them by Your truth. Your word is truth."

JOHN 17:15, 17 NKJV

FROM THE BEAUTY KIT

The word *lie* describes a situation where someone deliberately tells something that isn't true. *Light* shines into a dark space and illuminates it.

My friend, Emme, is classically beautiful. Her sweet spirit makes her even lovelier. She's always fashionably attired, and she has a favorite store where she loves to shop. She was delighted when they had a 70% off sale. Emme ordered several outfits, but they didn't fit when they arrived. She was surprised. She'd always worn that size from that store.

Emme was so upset that she called and expressed her disappointment. "You must be getting these clothes made elsewhere. Do you have a new manufacturer?" When the clerk replied they didn't, Emme said, "There must be a defect. I'm going to have to return them. I'm so disappointed your sizes have changed."

Soon after that, Emme made a discovery. It happened when she stepped on the scales and discovered that *she* was what had changed, because there were ten more pounds on the display than what had been there in the past. Emme called the store and apologized, "I just got off the scales, and it seems I'm the problem, not your clothes."

> When we make the discovery that we are not living in the image of God, the problem isn't him, it's us.

Emme had believed the wrong thing. We so often do the same thing, don't we?

The truth is that God says we're beautiful. We need to believe that, but there's a responsibility to our beauty, and sometimes we make choices that make us less than beautiful on the inside. When we make the discovery that we are not living in the image of God, the problem isn't him, it's us. Just as Emme learned that it wasn't the clothes at her favorite store that had changed, we need to take a long look at the mirror of our lives and discover how *we* have changed, and what has caused us to live less like Jesus.

Sometimes circumstances have rocked our worlds. Other times we've become so busy that God has been pushed to the side. Perhaps insecurity, feelings of inadequacy, or words have wounded us, causing us to shut everyone out, or to get mad at God. These are lies we must hold captive to the light of Jesus so we can be healed.

Have you ever had a facial at a salon? They do skin care by providing a deep cleansing process that removes impurities from the face. Often, the esthetician can correct things we're doing wrong, and can give great advice to avoid future problems by helping us deal with inflammation or other issues. Healthy glowing skin gives us confidence and makes us feel better about ourselves.

It's similar with God's soul care. First, he does a deep cleanse in our hearts, removing the impurities. Then through the light of his Word, he highlights the things we need to change, applying Scripture to areas where our hearts have been inflamed by Satan's lies. We can then go out each day with faces that glow with his love and the confidence that we have value and worth because we are his precious and beautiful creations.

Jesus, I often listen to other voices instead of listening to you. I give weight to what they say, and I brush off what you tell me, even though you're the one who loves me most. Give me courage to overcome the lies about my identity that have taken root in my heart, and help me to find my value and worth in you. As I go about my day, remind me that my body and soul are so marvelously made by you. Help me to see the lessons that you're teaching me, and to use those to help others see that they were created with hope and purpose. Amen.

BEAUTY QUESTIONNAIRE

1. Why are you so quick to believe the wrong things, to believe the lies?
2. What lie do you need to forgive and heal from? What truth do you need to believe?
3. How can you help others through what you've experienced?

GET YOUR STILETTOS MOVING

Think of three lies someone has told you that you've hung on to or that you've believed about yourself. Now bring them into the light of God's Word and apply his truth to those lies. Plan some "be still" time with God. Listen carefully to his voice and ask him what he wants you to hear.

THE MIRROR OF YOUR HEART

I WILL REPLACE THE LIES WITH GOD'S TRUTH.

How does it affect the mirror of your heart to know that lies will bring you heartache and God's truth will bring you joy?

_____

_____

_____

_____

_____

_____

_____

Chapter Twelve

WOUNDED TO WORTHY

He heals the brokenhearted and binds up their wounds.
PSALM 147:3 NIV

FROM THE BEAUTY KIT

The word *heal* means to cure someone or to restore them back to health, either physically or emotionally. The word *brokenhearted* refers to someone who is filled with despair or hurt, stricken with grief or heavy-hearted.

I met a man many years ago. (We'll call him Jared and his wife Beth.) Jared was exceptionally good-looking. He was tall, blonde, and could have been a male model. Add to it that he was successful, loved the Lord, and had a wonderful personality, and he was a great catch.

Several months after my husband and I met Jared, we were invited to dinner with him and his wife at the home of some friends. I hope my jaw didn't drop when Jared walked in with his wife that night. She was *so* not what I'd imagined. I was expecting the female equivalent of Jared—a Barbie type with great fashion sense, a cute figure, gorgeous hair, and perfect features.

Instead, Beth was chubby like me. Her hair didn't have any particular style to it, and she didn't have features that would make her stand out from anyone. But, oh my, when we sat down and talked, I discovered she was one of the most precious people I'd ever met. She was sweet and funny; she kept us all laughing. It was obvious that she and Jared were deeply in love.

On the way home that night, I told my husband, "She was nothing like what I expected."

He replied, "Oh, didn't I tell you? His first wife was gorgeous. Looked like a model. He fell hard for her, but after they were married, she was mean to him. She mistreated him, and if everything wasn't about her, she screamed and called him ugly names. She tore down his self-esteem and completely broke his heart."

> Jesus says, "I look at you and say you are valuable. I look at you and say you are loved. I look at you and say you are worthy."

That was so sad to me. My husband continued, "When he looked for a second wife, he didn't focus on outward beauty. He looked for someone who was beautiful on the inside. Someone who would love him and God." Jared found a beautiful treasure in Beth.

Perhaps some of you have been in situations where your heart has been broken, where you've been wounded and scarred emotionally, and sometimes physically. The big question is: How can you be fully healed where you're no longer reliving the pain each day?

Take some time and look for the root of your pain. Is it

rejection, fear of failure, betrayal, being taken advantage of, malicious hurt, or the absence of love that truly breaks your heart?

The good news is that Jesus is here to heal you in all these areas. You might have been wounded from putting your value and trust in another person. People will fail you. Your love needs to come from Jesus. Your value and your worth needs to come from him.

Jesus says, "I look at you and say you are valuable. I look at you and say you are loved. I look at you and say you are worthy." Begin your healing process by believing these truths from the God who loves you just as you are.

Dear Jesus, the pain of my past overwhelms me sometimes. The angry words that were yelled at me took root in my heart and grew a garden of bitterness. Rejection has affected my ability to feel loved and trampled my self-esteem. I don't want to live the rest of my life being bitter. I don't want to push people away when they try to love me. Today I bring my pain and bitterness to you. Heal me, Lord. Instead of listening to others, help me to listen to your loving voice and to find my worth in you. Amen.

BEAUTY QUESTIONNAIRE

1. What circumstances have broken your heart and how has that affected you?
2. Why is it more important to look at inward beauty rather than outer beauty?
3. How does God promise to help you in your healing process?

GET YOUR STILETTOS MOVING

One of the first things you must do to begin the healing process is to forgive the person who has hurt you. That's hard to do, but bitterness only hurts you. Ask God to help you forgive, then make a list of your hurts and bring them in prayer to the one who can heal your broken heart.

THE MIRROR OF YOUR HEART

JESUS HEALS THE BROKENHEARTED.

What does the mirror of your heart reflect when you think about Jesus healing your broken heart?

_____

_____

_____

_____

_____

_____

_____

I AM
A JOYFUL GIVER

Our mouths were filled with laughter, our tongues with songs of joy. Then it was said among the nations, "The LORD has done great things for them." The LORD has done great things for us, and we are filled with joy.

PSALM 126:2-3 NIV

I am generous.

I am joyful.

I am a joyful giver.

True beauty is serving others.

I use my gifts to serve others.

I am attractive because
I engage in acts of love.

As each one has received a gift, minister it to one another, as good stewards of the manifold grace of God.

1 PETER 4:10 NKJV

Chapter Thirteen

BEAUTIFUL GENEROSITY

*Let each one give as he purposes in his heart, not grudgingly
or of necessity; for God loves a cheerful giver.*
2 Corinthians 9:7 nkjv

FROM THE BEAUTY KIT

The word *generous* describes a person who gives willingly
and joyfully, and sometimes even sacrificially.

When asked to picture a beautiful woman, we don't usually
think of an elderly lady with wrinkles, no makeup, and gray hair
pulled up into a bun. For me, Lucy Stewart (usually called Maw
Stewart) was one of the most beautiful women I've ever known.
We went to church together. I was about twelve when I first met
her, and she had one of those personalities that radiated joy and
Jesus.

Many years ago, our church was on a pay-as-you-go policy to
build our new sanctuary. The congregation was small, but its faith
was big.

The supply company wouldn't unload the lumber or other materials until the load was paid for. Some Sundays, the pastor took up two or three offerings until we got what we needed. Then came the Sunday when Maw Stewart put her social security check in the offering plate. It was her only income. The pastor begged her to take it back, but she told him God would supply for her. That happened multiple times, and God took care of her every time. I'll never forget her joy as she gave and her beautiful heart that was so willing to sacrifice for what was precious to her.

When we serve Jesus with joy and give with generous hearts, it's a beautiful thing. It will touch the hearts of others for generations to come.

Fifty years later, the church is thriving, and the congregation has moved into a building three times that size. The church has a national television ministry and a presence worldwide. It supports missionaries around the world, cares for members in need, reaches out to the community, and began an emergency response organization that's helped people around the world. Countless people have come to know Jesus, and thousands of lives have been impacted for eternity.

Maw Stewart's willing sacrifice was part of all of this happening.

I hope I never forget the life lesson that precious lady taught me. Her example strengthened my faith. Her joy when giving sacrificially inspired a flame inside me to do the same. Her confidence that God would take care of her provided a beautiful example for all of us. She gave willingly, not so others could see, but as unto the Lord. He used her faithfulness to spur others to give, and because of that, the church building was completed.

Do we give willingly when God nudges our hearts, or do we remain tight-fisted as we hang onto what we think is ours? Everything that we have comes from God anyway, and the only thing we really have to give him is a willing heart. Being generous with our giving brings us one step closer to being able to physically control what we do to become beautiful women of God.

As Lucy Stewart proved, when we serve Jesus with joy and when we give with generous hearts, it's a beautiful thing. It will touch the hearts of others for generations to come.

Dear Jesus, thank you for the reminder that everything I have comes from you. Give me a heart that's generous to give back to you. I could never repay you for all you've done for me. You've given me so much and I thank you for blessing me. Forgive me for the times when I've been stingy with what I have. Give me a heart that finds joy in giving, even when it requires sacrifice on my part. When others look at my life, help them to see a woman with a beautiful, tender heart who gives whenever you whisper to her soul. Amen.

BEAUTY QUESTIONNAIRE

1. Why does God love a cheerful giver?
2. Why do you try to hang on to what is yours when God asks you to give something?
3. How can a generous spirit make you a beautiful woman of God?

GET YOUR STILETTOS MOVING

This might be a tough one. Today we want you to be generous to someone, whether it's with your money, time, or talents. Ask God to place someone on your heart who has a need, and then fulfill that need for them. It won't take long for you to discover something important: it's impossible to out-give God.

THE MIRROR OF YOUR HEART

What does the mirror of your heart
reflect about having a generous spirit?

_____

_____

_____

_____

_____

_____

_____

Chapter Fourteen

THE BEST MAKEUP

A merry heart makes a cheerful countenance.
PROVERBS 15:13 NKJV

FROM THE BEAUTY KIT

The word *merry* means full of joy. It describes someone
whose *countenance* (face) often has a warm smile or
an expression filled with laughter.

Tad and Pat Marshall had been married for twenty years. They
grieved that they couldn't have children. They'd given up hope and
moved on, immersing themselves in ministry with the teens at
their church. I'd seen Pat's sadness, so I began praying for a child
for them.

One day, the most amazing thing happened. A family member
of one of the girls in their youth group became pregnant. As a
young mom without any resources, she knew she couldn't keep the
child. She asked if Tad and Pat would be willing to adopt the baby.

After getting over the shock and praying about it, they replied
with a resounding yes. Over the next months, they attended

doctor appointments with the birth mom, and then the never-to-be-forgotten moment arrived when their baby was born.

The day they brought their new son home from the hospital, I drove to their house to meet little Tyler. As I walked in the door, Pat was bent over the bassinet picking him up. She turned toward me with her tiny miracle in her arms, and my first thought was, *Joy is the best cosmetic in the world.*

Joy is the best cosmetic in the world.

Pat glowed that day. I'd never seen her that beautiful. Sheer joy lit her eyes. Her smile sparkled, and a soft blush of happiness lit her face. Yes, it was definitely the best cosmetic ever.

We work so hard at our beauty routines. Yet for most of us, when we look in a mirror, we see our outward appearance and we're vastly disappointed as our flaws are magnified instead of our good points. A bad hair or face day can often ruin an otherwise good day. But here's the thing about that: while we focus on the outward appearance, God looks at our hearts.

Our days would become much more victorious if we focused on our hearts. How do we do that? Through finding joy.

Joy, peace, and confidence are some of our most attractive attributes, and those traits are what will draw others to us and ultimately to God. A great way to fill ourselves with joy is to start by singing praise to God. Close your eyes and listen to the words. Worship him.

Music lifts our souls, but we must have open and willing hearts to feel the freedom. We should pray and specifically ask God to fill us with joy. Then we need to find a way to be joyful givers of the gifts God has given us to glorify him. We can allow our outward appearance to reflect his love, joy, and peace because that beauty is contagious.

As Pat Marshall discovered, there's no better cosmetic than a face that reflects the joy of the Lord.

Dear Jesus, I want your beauty to shine from me, but I often make the wrong choices and end up spending the bulk of my time on me instead of you. Fill me with a resounding joy that will overflow my spirit, and fill my heart with your peace that surpasses understanding. Instead of beauty that will fade, let these attributes be what I seek. Help others to see your joy in me. Make me contagious. I want my life to sing your praises, to be a melody of joy to a world that needs to hear and see it. Amen.

BEAUTY QUESTIONNAIRE

1. Why do you spend so much time focusing on your outer appearance and so little time focusing on the inward attributes that will make you truly beautiful?
2. How can joy be one of the best cosmetics?
3. What are two things you can do to share God's joy with someone who needs to experience it?

GET YOUR STILETTOS MOVING

Sing a joy-filled song of praise. Sing it unto the Lord. Let the words sink into your heart and mind, and then make a list of the ways God has brought you joy.

THE MIRROR OF YOUR HEART

I AM JOYFUL.

What does the mirror of your heart reflect about joy?

_____

_____

_____

_____

_____

_____

_____

Chapter Fifteen

GIVING WITH JOY

*Each of you should give what you have decided in
your heart to give, not reluctantly or under compulsion,
for God loves a cheerful giver.*

2 Corinthians 9:7 niv

FROM THE BEAUTY KIT

The word *joyful* means happy and cheerful.
Joy is contagious, especially when it comes from hearts
that are full of Jesus. The word *giver* describes someone
who gives or provides something or performs tasks
for someone else.

The missionary's slide show stopped at one of the photos as he
shared a story. The Christmas before, someone had bought bottles
of soft drinks for the children at an orphanage in Malawi, and it
was such a special treat that the children made them last for days.

That story brought tears to Rhea's eyes. The next Christmas,
and every year since, she has supplied soft drinks for the orphans
and staff. She and her husband went on to pay for Christmas

dinner for the orphanage each year after that.

It's their favorite Christmas gift to give and they do it joyfully. One year when the missionary sent a photo of the group with their plates of Christmas dinner, holding their bottles of soft drinks, it made Rhea and her husband cry.

When Teresa heard about a college student who didn't have money to buy food, she went to the store and bought all that she thought he'd need for his meals. To save his pride, she dropped it by the church office and they called the young man to come in. It moved Teresa to tears when she heard that he cried as he saw all the bags of food that were waiting for him.

> The simple fact that we have something to give means that God has blessed us with an abundance.

Many years ago, Paula went to a small church. When she noticed her pastor's shoes had holes in the bottom, she bought him a new pair, wrapped them up, and added a verse from Isaiah 52:7, "How lovely on the mountains are the feet of him who brings good news." She left the box sitting on his front porch. It made her smile the next Sunday when she saw him preaching with his shiny new shoes.

Friends, there is joy in giving—not just for the recipient, but for those who do the giving as well. The simple fact that we have something to give means that God has blessed us with an abundance whether it's time, talents, or money.

Sometimes we resist when God asks us to give. At times, he asks us to give sacrificially or give up something that is precious to us. That's when we need to look deep into our souls to see if we have selfish hearts that love ourselves more than others.

Denying God's requests to give will always bring shame and

guilt to our souls, but being obedient to those nudges will always bring joy and blessing. There's pure beauty in a woman who gives cheerfully and willingly.

How we should give is also important. We should give as if we were giving the gifts to the Lord. We should give without any expectation of getting anything in return except a big smile from Jesus in our hearts. It's impossible to give with joy without receiving joy in return.

A woman who gives with a heart full of joy will be beautiful to her Savior and all who know her.

Lord, make me sensitive to those who need a helping hand. When I'm selfish with what I have, remind me that all of it comes from you. Whether it's my time, talents, or dollars, help me to give joyfully as unto you. Thank you for the ones who have given so much to me and my family, some of them giving sacrificially. Bless them for being a blessing to us, and help me to be a blessing to others. Give me eyes that see the needs of others, knees that will bend in prayer for those needs, and a heart that will put feet to my prayers as I share with joy from the countless blessings you've given me. Amen.

BEAUTY QUESTIONNAIRE

1. What are some specific ways God has blessed you?
2. Why is how we give important?
3. Why does giving with a joyful heart make a difference?

GET YOUR STILETTOS MOVING

Ask God to show you two people or ministries that have needs. Ask him how he wants you to be part of supplying those needs. Maybe it's helping a ministry paint their offices, or sending a care package to missionaries. Perhaps it's a monetary gift or mentoring new brides or young moms. Give with joy, and then watch God double your joy as you see the results of what you've given.

THE MIRROR OF YOUR HEART

I AM A JOYFUL GIVER.

What does the mirror of your heart reflect when you give joyfully as unto the Lord?

_____

_____

_____

_____

_____

_____

Chapter Sixteen

TRUE BEAUTY

*God is not unjust so as to forget your work and the love which
you have shown toward His name, in having ministered and
in still ministering to the saints.*

HEBREWS 6:10

FROM THE BEAUTY KIT

The word *true* describes something that is real.
The word *beauty* describes exceptional loveliness or
something that is pleasing and inspiring. The word *serve*
describes the act of helping those in need.

Jacque Sexton was a beautiful woman by any standards. In
her younger years, she was petite with dark hair, fair skin, a lovely
figure, and sparkling blue eyes. Add her sweet smile and fun
personality, and she always stood out in a crowd. The passing of
years had frosted her hair white, a few pounds had crept on, and
smile lines had settled on her face, but she was still beautiful. She
wasn't a blood relation, but in every way that mattered, Nana was
family to me.

Whenever I think of her, Nana's beauty isn't what usually

comes to mind. I remember her warmth, the welcome and the heartfelt hug that always waited on me whenever we were together. I remember talking to her about what was going on in my life and receiving sage advice from a woman who'd spent her life chasing after Jesus. I remember her laughter, her sense of mischief, and how much fun it was to be with her and Poppie.

True beauty is serving others.

—BELLE WINTERS
THE FARMER AND
THE BELLE: SAVING
SANTALAND

Most of all, I remember the way she lived each day—with kindness and compassion, with love for those whom others would consider unlovable, and with the way she forgave people who wounded her deeply.

Nana was a pastor's wife who took her role seriously, and she passed out love as easily as she did heaping helpings of her oh-so-delicious dinners. She had a servant's heart, and helping others brought her as much joy as she delivered to them.

When we put others first, the beauty of Jesus shines off us and it's contagious.

Jenn met a woman who'd been disfigured, but the joy of the Lord made her the most attractive woman she'd ever met. An aesthetically pretty girl stood next to her, but over and over again, Jenn watched as people were attracted to the disfigured girl. And then it dawned on her. They were attracted to the sweetness of Jesus that reflected from her as she served those around her.

Both of these women had discovered something important: true beauty is serving others with a joyful heart and doing it as unto the Lord. Both impacted others with their unconditional love, pure hearts, and the fact that neither of them expected anything in return.

Here's the thing; some of us might never be outwardly

beautiful. It's a level playing field when it comes to having a servant's heart for others. That might include a simple smile to someone having a hard day, kind words to a weary cashier, or loading packages into the trunk for someone with physical limitations. Perhaps it's a hug for a friend going through a difficult time, giving a gift to encourage someone, raking the leaves for a senior citizen, or spending quality time with someone who is lonely.

You'll never regret having a servant's heart. God, and others, will look at you and see a woman of truly exceptional beauty.

Father, there are so many people around me who need to feel your love. Give me a servant's heart and make me tender to the heartaches of those with whom I come in contact. I know that true beauty comes in serving others. Give me a spirit of compassion and a servant's heart. Help me to minister to the sick, to love those who are starving for someone to care. Make me a hospital of hope to a world that needs it. Help my life to be a beautiful example of your love for us, and help me to always put you first. Amen.

BEAUTY QUESTIONNAIRE

1. How can you reflect the beauty of Jesus? Why do others notice that?
2. What is a servant's heart, and how does that affect you and others?
3. What happens when you put Jesus first? How can that change your life?

GET YOUR STILETTOS MOVING

Make a list of three people who need to have the love of Jesus extended to them. Write down some specific ways you can have a servant's heart for them. Now do it! Afterwards, write down how it affected you and how it impacted them.

THE MIRROR OF YOUR HEART

TRUE BEAUTY IS SERVING OTHERS.

What does the mirror of your heart reflect about you serving others?

_____

_____

_____

_____

_____

_____

_____

Chapter Seventeen

GIFTED FOR GLORY

*Each of you should use whatever gift you have
received to serve others, as faithful stewards
of God's grace in its various forms.*
1 PETER 4:10 NIV

FROM THE BEAUTY KIT

The word *gifts* describes the talents or skills God has given us. The word *works* refers to the efforts, acts, or labor that we do. *Glory* is the honor and praise that we can bring to God through using the gifts and talents he has built into us.

If you could see my cute friend, Carol, with her bubbly personality and fashion flair, the last thing you'd ever imagine is that the Bling Queen would do ministry at a men's prison. But she does. Her personality, warmth, and her love for God has enabled her to reach the hearts of hardened criminals in a special way that he designed just for her.

Nobody ever walked through the doors of Trinity Baptist and felt unwelcome as long as Macie Bailey was around. This precious elderly lady met folks at the door each Sunday, wrapping each person in a warm hug as she said, "I'm so glad you-uns are here today!" Then she'd make her rounds, giving away hugs throughout the congregation. Her love brought smiles, especially to first-time visitors. Her God-given talent as a people-greeter was a blessing to all of us.

For many years, my friend Dee Dee fixed homemade soup, packed it in Mason jars, and delivered it to sick friends, those with family members in the hospital, folks who'd lost a loved one, or anyone else who needed a little love. God gave her the gift of encouraging others.

> Whatever we do, when we do it as unto the Lord and do it joyfully, it brings glory to him and blesses others.

Girlfriends, these might not be big talents like being a Grammy Award-winning singer or an accomplished artist, but *every* gift God gives us is important to his purposes, and if we don't use those gifts and talents, they go to waste.

How can we joyfully give of our talents to serve others? It begins with identifying what we're good at. What are we passionate about? What makes us smile? What do we enjoy?

Some of you might be shaking your heads as you say, "I really don't have a talent." I guarantee that you do. Maybe it's making someone smile. Perhaps it's bringing comfort and sharing God's precious promises with someone who's hurting.

Can you cook? Teach a Sunday school class? Do mechanical or household repairs for a single mom? Send cards of encouragement to missionaries? Can you sing in the choir? Could you use your writing or acting talents for God? Can you send money to buy gifts for an orphanage? Could you give your time to be with someone who's lonely? Perhaps you could clean a house for a senior citizen who has trouble doing that anymore. Or maybe you have social media or photography skills that you could use for a Christian ministry.

In the movie *The Farmer and the Belle: Saving Santaland,* the lead character Belle Winters finds her family's heirloom bracelet she lost when she was a child and discovers true beauty is serving others. There is an inscription on her bracelet's charm that says, "Use whatever gift you received to serve others." "Make yourself attractive by doing acts of love." These words propel Belle to unveil her talents with joy as she saves her childhood pen pal's Santaland.

You see, *whatever* we do, when we do it as unto the Lord and do it joyfully, it brings glory to God and blesses others. What could be more special than using our talents to please God, and having a heart that is beautiful and willing to fulfill his purposes?

Father, show me the gifts and talents you've given me, even the things that seem so little that I've never considered them a gift before. I'm humbled that you've blessed me with these things, and I want to use all of them for you. Show me opportunities where I can serve. Make me sensitive to the needs of others. Let the beauty of Jesus flow through me and help me to use my gifts and talents to tell others about our amazing and loving God. Help whatever I do to bring glory to you. Amen.

BEAUTY QUESTIONNAIRE

1. What are the talents you could use for God?
2. What individuals or ministries might need those talents?
3. How can using your talents bring glory to God?

GET YOUR STILETTOS MOVING

Make a list of three talents or gifts God has given you. Spend some time in prayer asking God how he wants you to use those for him. Do three tasks using those talents, and then write down how it makes you feel. Somehow, whenever we do things for God, we're the ones who truly end up blessed.

THE MIRROR OF YOUR HEART

USE WHATEVER GIFT YOU HAVE RECEIVED TO SERVE OTHERS.

What does the mirror of your heart reflect when you use your gifts and talents for the Lord?

_____

_____

_____

_____

_____

_____

_____

Chapter Eighteen

BECAUSE I LOVE YOU

*"A new commandment I give to you,
that you love one another, even as I have loved you,
that you also love one another."*

JOHN 13:34

FROM THE BEAUTY KIT

The word *attractive* describes someone or something that is
charming or lovely in a manner that draws people in.
Acts of love are things done for others without any expectation
for payment or recognition.

The evening was momentous. My husband and I had headed
out for dinner and our weeknight date to do some shopping and
go to the grocery store. That wasn't what was momentous, though.

What made the evening exceptional was that after I'd done
my makeup, flat-ironed my hair, and got dressed for our night out,
I looked in the mirror and uttered a surprised, "Wow, I actually
look pretty good today." I'm talented when it comes to seeing all
my flaws, so I enjoyed walking out the door with my favorite guy

while strains of "I Feel Good" floated through my head.

We finished the evening at the grocery store. Way down the aisle, I noticed a lady we'd known for many years. She's about fifteen years younger than me, and I've always thought she was so pretty. But this night, she looked like she was twenty years older than me. She was hunched over, shuffling along as if she could barely walk. I was stunned.

A few minutes later, when we were close enough to speak, she looked at me and said, "Well, bless your heart, honey. You look like I feel."

Oh, sweet mercy! I looked like *that*? And here I'd thought I looked good. Let's just say when I left the building that evening, I was not the same confident gal who went into the store.

I laugh about it now. It truly was a funny moment. But you know what? All of us will have days we don't feel attractive. When we're having a bad hair day. Or a bad face day. Or even a bad body day. But we can always be attractive when we're loving those around us, doing it with joy to please the Lord, and not expecting to gain recognition in return.

We can always be attractive when we're loving those around us, doing it with joy to please the Lord, and not expecting any recognition or payment in return.

We can serve with joy when we pay attention to God's nudges. He might put someone on our hearts, or we might take time to discover what makes our family or friends feel loved. We could give them a thoughtful gift, spend time with them, say the words they need to hear, or even encourage them with a hug.

Jenn's husband likes acts of service. This is the farthest thing away from how Jenn's brain responds. So, she has to think extra hard to consider her husband's needs above hers and find ways to serve. Folding clothes, making a snack, or providing something he needs fuels his love tank. Physical touch communicates love to Jenn. When her husband puts a hand on her leg while they drive, it makes her feel loved.

Friends, what could be more attractive than acts of love? They're guaranteed to never go out of style, and they will always please the heart of God.

Father, I take pleasure in the days I feel attractive. Help me to be more concerned about having a heart that's attractive for you because that's what will matter for eternity. Help me to love my family and friends, to search for what makes them feel loved, and to share that love joyfully to them as you have so often done for me. Help me to look for others who are starved for someone to care about them, even when it's sometimes difficult to love them. Remind me to do it for your glory and not for me to get recognition or applause. Amen.

BEAUTY QUESTIONNAIRE

1. How can you pay attention when God nudges you to show love to someone?
2. Why are acts of love attractive?
3. Why is it important to serve others with joy?

GET YOUR STILETTOS MOVING

Ask God to put three people on your heart this week. Identify what makes them feel special, and then do an act of love for each of them. After you've done that, spend some quiet time with God and ask him this question, "Lord, what can I do for you that will make *you* feel loved?"

THE MIRROR OF YOUR HEART

MAKE YOURSELF ATTRACTIVE BY DOING ACTS OF LOVE.

What does the mirror of your heart reflect about your acts of love toward others?

_____

_____

_____

_____

_____

_____

_____

I AM OBEDIENT TO MY CALLING

*Jesus looked at them and said, "With man this is impossible,
but with God all things are possible."*

I am courageous.

I am obedient to my calling.

God gives me talents for his glory.

With God all things are possible.

God has plans to prosper me.

God has plans not to harm me.

*"For I know the plans I have for you," declares the Lord,
"plans to prosper you and not to harm you,
plans to give you hope and a future."*

Chapter Nineteen

WOMAN OF COURAGE

"Have I not commanded you? Be strong and courageous! Do not tremble or be dismayed, for the LORD your God is with you wherever you go."

JOSHUA 1:9

FROM THE BEAUTY KIT

The word *courage* describes the trait of doing something we are afraid of, stepping out in faith into uncertain circumstances. The word *strong* denotes a person who can carry heavy objects or someone who is tough emotionally. The word *confident* reflects a person's self-assurance or their trust in their own or someone else's abilities.

My favorite place in public is on the back row. Being in front of people used to make me break out in a cold sweat. (You know, the horizontally-challenged thing, and the lack of fashion, and the bad hair… I could go on and on.) So wouldn't you know it, being in the public eye is exactly where God has placed me. I've sometimes been so far out of my comfort zone I've been in another comfort country!

A while back, my publicist emailed with news that I was booked for a nationwide television show (with my co-author). It was a wonderful opportunity, but my first thought was, *Yikes! What will I wear?* I've discovered something as I've done television appearances: there are different looks to various shows. Some are extra dressy, some require business attire, and some are more casual.

This appearance would be the expensive jeans and lovely top style. I set out on a frantic search in our small town and found nothing. I started to panic. The time was short and I had *nothing* to wear that was just right for this show. Fear started creeping in. You see, I've found that *feeling* like I look nice gives me courage and confidence.

> It's only when we take that first scary step of faith that we can become the beautiful creation God desires for us.

I did what I should have done much sooner. I prayed and said, "God will you please help me find something that I will feel nice in?" My husband and I drove to a larger town, walked into a store, and the first top I saw was exactly what I'd hoped to find. *And* they had the perfect jeans in my size.

A few weeks later, backed by prayer, armed with Jesus and my "just right" outfit, I had the courage and confidence to do the task God had called me to do.

Courage is something we all need as we walk through life. We need it to overcome life's difficulties, fears, and uncertainties. We need courage as we step forward into the unknown. Remember Peter's fears when he stepped out of the boat, stood on water, and walked to Jesus? That took courage, but his trust in Jesus made the difference.

Sweet friends, sometimes God asks us to do things for him

that fill us with fear. We don't see how we can possibly do them. We worry about all the things we'll need, or that we won't have the funding or the strength to do them. And we allow fear to keep us from accomplishing the tasks God has for us to do.

If God calls us to do something, he will equip us with all that we need. He will bless our efforts, and he will be with us for every moment of the journey.

It's only when we take that first scary step of faith that we can become the beautiful creation God desires for us. Will you take the first step for him today, courageous friend?

Father, I want to serve you, I want to be faithful, but I'm afraid. Next time fear tingles throughout my body, help me to remember that I am not alone—that you are with me. Remind me that fear is false evidence that just appears real, but that you have come to cast out all fear. Give me the courage and confidence to step out in faith and to chase the dreams you have for me. God, more than anything, I want to be the beautiful woman you want me to be, and I want to fulfill the plans you have for me. Amen.

BEAUTY QUESTIONNAIRE

1. How has fear kept you from stepping out in faith?
2. Why is prayer so important as you step out in faith to chase your dreams for God?
3. How can faith in God and courage equip you to become the beautiful woman of faith God desires you to be?

GET YOUR STILETTOS MOVING

What do you need courage to do? Envision Jesus doing it with you. Then make a list with two columns. In the first column, list the things that make you fearful or worried as you start to step out in faith. In the second column, list all the times in the Bible where it says that God failed.

THE MIRROR OF YOUR HEART

What does the mirror of your heart reflect about you becoming courageous?

_____

_____

_____

_____

_____

_____

_____

Chapter Twenty

OBEDIENT TO A CALLING

He said, "On the contrary, blessed are those
who hear the word of God and observe it."
LUKE 11:28 NASB

FROM THE BEAUTY KIT

The word *obedient* means to have a respectful and submissive
spirit that is willing to comply. The word *calling* refers to a
profession or mission that we're passionate about, in this instance,
something that God has asked us to do.

When I was first married, I had some lofty goals. I'd keep a
spotless house, serve delightful meals, finish all my work, and
would still look pretty and be charming every day when my
husband arrived home. It didn't take long for those unrealistic
expectations to crash like Humpty Dumpty from his wall,
especially when children arrived. After the babies came, there were
some days where combing my hair became a big accomplishment.
With the exhaustion and lack of time, I was anything but pretty.

Girlfriends, aren't we the world's worst when it comes to having crazy expectations for ourselves? And then there's that seemingly perfect Proverbs 31 woman in the Bible that we have to live up to. What's a gal to do?

After studying that Proverbs 31 woman, I discovered all of us could be like her if we were willing to be obedient to what God calls us to do. First, she's a good wife. Her husband trusts her because she does good things for him instead of evil ones.

God will be your provider, so step out in faith and confidence.

Second, she's a willing worker. This woman isn't lazy. She cares for her family, even when it requires rising early and staying up late. And she cares for the poor and needy.

Third, she uses her talents and skills. She plants a vineyard. She's a seamstress. And a merchant.

Fourth, she wears strength and honor like clothing. She's a woman of wisdom, her tongue expresses kindness, and she fears the Lord.

Because of all that, her children call her "blessed" and her husband praises her. I imagine God is pleased as well because she was obedient to her calling. She discovered that God is the one who takes our ordinary and changes it into extraordinary.

What is *your* calling? The best place to start is in prayer asking God to show you his unique design planned just for you. Then take a look at the skills and talents he has given you: those things that come naturally to you. What are your interests? Your passions? How can you use those to glorify him?

Consider journaling to help you sort it out. Once you've prayed and spent some quiet time with God, make a list of what you hear or feel from your prayer time, or the things he points out to you in his Word. God will show you the purpose he has for you.

The next step is moving out in faith to fulfill his calling for you. You won't be the Proverbs 31 woman, but you can learn from her. God wants *you*. If you'll be faithful to him and what he has called you to do, you can have just as much impact on your spouse, family, friends, and community, and just as big a testimony as she did. What could be more beautiful than that?

Dear Lord, I want to please you but I'm not sure what you want me to do with my life. Show me the perfect plan you have for me. Remove my fear and doubts and give me a road map to guide me on my way. Give me joy for the journey. I want to be obedient to what you call me to do and to fulfill that calling in a manner that will make you proud. Make my life a daily testimony of your faithfulness, and help me to someday stand in front of you to hear the words, "Well done, my good and faithful servant. You used every scrap of the talents I gave you." Amen.

BEAUTY QUESTIONNAIRE

1. What can you learn from the Proverbs 31 woman?
2. How can you discover what God has called you to do?
3. How does being obedient to your calling affect you and others?

GET YOUR STILETTOS MOVING

Make a list of your talents. God gave those to you and he has a reason for everything he does. Now make a list of your passions: the things that make your eyes light up when you talk about them. Finally, make a list of how these passions and talents could be used to glorify God and to fulfill your calling.

THE MIRROR OF YOUR HEART

I AM OBEDIENT TO MY CALLING.

What does the mirror of your heart reflect when you are obedient to your calling?

_____

_____

_____

_____

_____

_____

_____

Chapter Twenty-One

NO EXCUSES

As each one has received a gift, minister it to one another,
as good stewards of the manifold grace of God.
1 PETER 4:10 NKJV

FROM THE BEAUTY KIT

The word *gift* describes something that is given without having
to pay for it. The word *talent* refers to the gifts God has given like
a beautiful voice, writing or acting skills, a faithful prayer life,
the ability to encourage, or many other things. The word *glory*
describes the act of giving the praise, attention,
and credit to someone.

A number of years ago, I had a panic moment as I walked
through a large bookstore. I removed a book from the shelf and
pointed to the photo of the author on the back cover. "Lord, I can't
do what you're asking. I'm not beautiful like her." The conversation
continued down the aisle as I pulled out more books. "God, this
author is so talented. There's no way I can write like him." And
with the next book, "And she's so well-known. I'm a wife and

mom from the country. Nobody knows who I am." The excuses continued.

Not long before this, God had called me to write for him. I'd never even considered writing, and now I found myself in the bookstore using every excuse I could find to get out of it. I discovered that God had an answer for all my excuses: "I'm not beautiful like her. *Not a problem, then they'll notice me.* "I can't write like this talented author." *I already have one of him. I need one of you and I have equipped you with everything you need to write for me.* "Nobody knows who I am." *Well, they know who I am, and they need to know more about me.*

Okay, Lord, I get it now. You didn't call me to be successful, you called me to be faithful.

The difference in my attitude about my writing came when I took the focus off me and put it on him. When I knelt beside my couch and prayed, "Okay, Lord, I get it now. You didn't call me to be successful, you called me to be faithful." I realized that a willing heart was all he wanted from me, and that He'd take care of the rest. I could use my talents for his glory by giving them all to him.

This is where the trust factor comes in. Sometimes we have to step out in faith as if walking on a tightrope with our eyes on Jesus. If we look away, we'll get wobbly, but as long as we keep our eyes on him, we'll find the peace, provision, and strength that we need.

There's something else important to think about. Who are you doing things for? Do you want man's favor and praise or would you rather glorify God? Keep your eyes on him and remember that every bit of talent you have is a gift from God.

Today would be the perfect time to take that first scary step of faith. Wouldn't it be a shame for the talents that God gave you to go to waste? What could be better than becoming a beautiful reflection of Jesus by using the talents that he gave you? Let him use your efforts so others can discover just how amazing he is.

Father, help me be a faithful steward of the gifts and talents you've given me. Thank you for providing all that I need and for equipping me for each task you've assigned. Remind me to use my talents for your glory instead of mine. Lord, I know that all talents are important to you, whether it's teaching a class, being a prayer warrior for others, acting in a movie, wiping little noses in the church nursery, or writing a book. Help me to hold on to the hope of your promises, knowing you have plans to prosper me and not to harm me. Help me to be a woman of beautiful faithfulness for you. Amen.

BEAUTY QUESTIONNAIRE

1. Why is it so scary to step out in faith?
2. Why is the first step important?
3. What talents has God given to you? How can you use those talents for him?

GET YOUR STILETTOS MOVING

Envision the throne of God and imagine him watching to see if you will use your talents for him. Will you bring joy to his face? Make a list of the talents he has given you and then make a list of how you can use those for his glory.

THE MIRROR OF YOUR HEART

GOD GIVES
TALENTS FOR
HIS GLORY.

What does the mirror of your heart reflect about using your talents for God?

_____

_____

_____

_____

_____

_____

_____

Chapter Twenty-Two

ALL THINGS POSSIBLE

Jesus looked at them and said, "With man this is impossible,
but with God all things are possible."
MATTHEW 19:26 NIV

FROM THE BEAUTY KIT

The word *possible* means something within reach, something
achievable. The word *impossible* describes something that isn't
going to happen, something that's so ridiculous and unachievable
there isn't any hope of it happening. The word *all* means
everything or the entirety or totality of something.

My sweet friend, Jenn, is beautiful inside and out. One of
the things I've been privileged to watch is the beauty of her being
obedient to the calling God has placed on her heart.

A while back Jenn was cast in the movie *Hulk* filming in San
Francisco. God spoke to her the night before filming began at a
worship service: "With God all things are possible."

The next morning as she drove to the set, Jenn prayed, "God,
let me be a light on set. Let me love others like you love me, and

let me have lines." And then, since she'd been cast as a background actor with no lines, she muttered, "Yeah, right. That's impossible."

Conviction hit her then, so she almost jokingly said, "With God all things are possible. If you want me to have lines, Lord, it's in your hands." She let go of that prayer as a balloon with helium releases into the air. Four hours later, she was on set and the director asked if she'd like to say something in the scene. She was no longer an extra, but considered principal cast and invited to eat lunch with the cast to prepare for the next scene in the restaurant.

> God loves it when our faith exceeds our fears.

When you watch the movie, you'll see her hands in the Officers Club scene when the waitress (her character) approaches the table of main actors, and you'll hear her lines. The exact answer to the prayer she'd muttered.

I suspect all of us look at situations in our lives as impossible. God whispers that he wants us to do something for him, and the first words out of our mouths are, "That's not possible. There's no way that will happen." We limit God by looking at our *limited* abilities instead of focusing on his *limitless* abilities.

When God says something more than once in the Bible, he obviously wants us to pay attention to it. He does that several times as he tells us that all things are possible with him, and nothing is impossible.

Do you believe the truth God tells us in his Word—the instruction manual he left for us? When we surrender and put our hearts, tears, and peers into his hands, we can soar for him.

God loves it when our faith exceeds our fears. He doesn't want us to doubt or worry or have anything that takes us away from being intimate with him. How do we do this? We pray. We ask

God for bigger faith. And we replace each fearful lie with his truth, "With God *all* things are possible."

Take those first steps of faith. Surrender the desires of your heart into God's hands. Ask him what you need to do and then trust him. Step out with courage and confidence because your strength is found in God and *all* things are possible when he's in control.

Dear Lord, I look at some of the big dreams I want to accomplish for you, and then the doubts and fears take over. Give me a beautiful faith. Cast out all my doubts and let me stand on your holy ground in the truth that with you all things are possible. I give you my heart's desires, my wants, and my fears. Give me the boldness and courage to move into your calling for my life. Make the path clear and help me to follow in your footsteps throughout each day. I can and will succeed because you are in charge and you have never failed me. Amen.

BEAUTY QUESTIONNAIRE

1. What are some seemingly impossible situations in your life?
2. Why do you focus on your limited abilities instead of God's limitless ones?
3. How can your faith exceed your fears?

GET YOUR STILETTOS MOVING

What are some big tasks you want to accomplish for God? Make a list. Start praying about specific requests for each of those tasks and write them down on your list. At the top of the list, write *With God All Things Are Possible*. Every few months, go back and look at your list and requests. You will be amazed, and your faith will be bolstered, when you see what God has done.

THE MIRROR OF YOUR HEART

WITH GOD
ALL THINGS
ARE POSSIBLE.

What does the mirror of your heart reflect when you truly realize that *nothing* is impossible for God?

_____

_____

_____

_____

_____

_____

Chapter Twenty-Three

MADE PROSPEROUS

"The LORD your God will make you most prosperous in all the work of your hands and in the fruit of your womb, the young of your livestock and the crops of your land. The LORD will again delight in you and make you prosperous, just as he delighted in your ancestors."

DEUTERONOMY 30:9 NIV

FROM THE BEAUTY KIT

The word *plans* describes the process of conceiving ideas and developing strategies to implement them. The word *prosper* refers to occasions when we are successful, thrive, or become wealthy.

If we're honest, most of us have had a time or two when we were envious of what someone else had. We see the beautiful jetsetters in their designer fashions with expensive purses. We read about their trips to exotic locations, their glamorous lifestyles, or even the prestige or attention they receive because of their wealth, and then we go back to the drudgery of our days as we juggle jobs, laundry, family, bills, and a gazillion other things.

Sometimes we become discontented with the blessings that God has given us, or we even fail to see those blessings. And at times, some of us might have even complained, moaned, groaned, or had a prolonged pity party.

At times, we don't feel worthy of having God prosper us, but we are his beloved children and that makes us valuable and worthy.

The truth is that God *wants* us to prosper. The Bible even says that he delights in us just as he delighted in our ancestors. It says that just like a father loves to give to his children, he enjoys giving us good gifts. God loves for us to bring our needs and dreams to him. When our requests reflect a desire to do things for him, it touches his heart.

It doesn't necessarily mean we're going to become financially wealthy, thin, beautiful, or have folks hanging on our every word, but it does mean that he will bless the work of our hands, our families, and our lives. He often does it in ways that will surprise and astound us. Just as it does an earthly father, it gives God joy to see us happy. We can bring all our requests to him because his resources are limitless.

At the end of our lives, even if our bank accounts don't end with lots of zeroes, we can look back at a life spent with Jesus and know that we have been truly wealthy, and that he has blessed and prospered us beyond words.

There's a reason for God to prosper us: so we can serve him more. When he blesses our families, he gives us peace and happiness in our homes and plants his love and character in the lives of our children. There truly is no greater joy than to see our children serving God and to serve alongside them. A beautiful woman of faith with a family who loves the Lord is wealthy indeed.

When God blesses us financially, we can give more to missions and to church, and we can help others who are going through difficult times. There's a sweet delight when we can help others, and often we get more out of it than they do.

When God blesses us with prestige or public honor, it's a way for us to tell others about our amazing God, how he has blessed us, and about the difference he has made in our lives. It's for his glory.

At the end of our lives, even if our bank accounts don't end with lots of zeroes, we can look back at a life spent with Jesus and know that we have been truly wealthy, and that he has blessed and prospered us beyond words.

Dear Father, it humbles me that you want me to prosper. Sometimes I neglect to really stop and think about the abundance of the gifts, talents, relationships, and eternal life that you have given me. Just the fact that you love me makes me rich. You've made me wealthy in all the ways that really matter, and there are no words to express my gratitude. Help me to understand the depth of your magnificent love for me, and help me to use the blessings that you give me for things that truly matter. Amen.

BEAUTY QUESTIONNAIRE

1. Why do you sometimes fail to see the blessings God has given you?
2. What are some of the ways God has made you wealthy?
3. How can prosperity be used for God?

GET YOUR STILETTOS MOVING

What are some areas of your life where you'd like to prosper? Make a list. Make a second list of how you can use those things for God. Spend some time in prayer bringing your requests before your Father who loves you and delights in making you prosperous.

THE MIRROR OF YOUR HEART

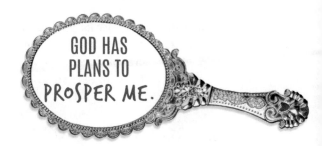

GOD HAS PLANS TO PROSPER ME.

What does the mirror of your heart reflect when you realize God wants you to prosper?

_____

_____

_____

_____

_____

_____

_____

Chapter Twenty-Four

GOD HAS PLANS

"For I know the plans I have for you," declares the Lord,
"plans to prosper you and not to harm you,
plans to give you hope and a future."

Jeremiah 29:11 niv

FROM THE BEAUTY KIT

The word *harm* refers to wounding, damaging, hurting, or
destroying someone or something.

I've loved to watch beauty pageants since I was a child. The
evening gowns are breathtaking. And the swimsuit competition?
How do they walk with such confidence in a bathing suit and
four-inch heels? The talent section can get interesting as women
perform a variety of acts. Stress levels often rise as the beauty
queens respond to questions they are given without advance time
to prepare. Some give wise and witty replies, and others have the
deer-in-the-headlights look as they search their minds for wisdom
that seems to have evaporated.

The pageant is fun to watch, but for the women in the

competition, it's serious—the culmination of thousands of dollars and months of work. Each of them has had a plan. They've exercised and dieted so their figures will be as perfect as possible. There have been intense searches for evening gowns that are flattering and have the wow factor. The women have practiced hairstyles and makeup numerous times to achieve just the right look. They've had mock question-and-answer sessions to prepare for those moments. And they've practiced their talent until they could do it while sleeping.

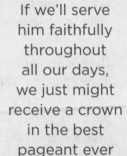

If we'll serve him faithfully throughout all our days, we just might receive a crown in the best pageant ever for a heart that is beautiful.

One thing has always fascinated me as I've watched the programs: there's usually one woman whose sweetness is apparent throughout the evening. Some have gotten vain during the process, and it's evident in their demeanor. There's a side of the pageant that isn't seen on TV: the display of jealousy behind the scenes. On occasion, makeup or clothing is sabotaged in hopes of ruining the chances of another contestant.

It's hard to believe that a woman would try to harm someone just to be successful in winning the crown, but that's what happens when inner beauty isn't there to match physical beauty.

Dear friends, most of us will never win a beauty competition, but we can seek to become exquisite for God. Just as those contestants worked hard to be their best on pageant day, we must do so spiritually. We'll need a steady diet of God's Word and time in prayer so our hearts can become lovely, and we'll need to use our talents so they are a wonderful display for God.

When we search diligently for Jesus, we'll find him, and then we can model a garment of his grace and mercy for others. When we allow him to give us the words to say, we'll never have to worry about giving the wrong answers.

And, unlike those beauty contestants, there's one thing we'll never have to concern ourselves with: God will not try to harm us along the way because he wants us to be successful. If we serve him faithfully throughout our days, we just might receive a crown in the best pageant ever for a heart that is beautiful.

Dear Jesus, sometimes I feel like the ugly duckling at the beauty pageant when it comes to serving you. I look at other women who are doing great things for you and I fall so short. But I realize that you didn't call me to be them, you called me to be me, and I want to be the best that I can be for you. How precious to know that you will never do anything to harm me, but you want to prosper me as I seek to serve you. More than anything, my heart desires for you to look at me and see a woman with a heart of exquisite beauty. Help me to live faithfully for you through every day of my life. Amen.

BEAUTY QUESTIONNAIRE

1. Why does God want you to be successful?
2. Why do you never have to worry about God harming you?
3. The beauty contestants had a plan. Why do you need a plan when it comes to serving Jesus?

GET YOUR STILETTOS MOVING

Make a plan today for what you need to do to become the spiritual beauty God desires. Do you need to pray, read his Word, or share his love more? Do you need to get rid of excess baggage that is weighing down your heart? Make your list and then choose three things to start with today.

THE MIRROR OF YOUR HEART

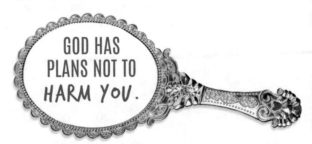

GOD HAS
PLANS NOT TO
HARM YOU.

What does the mirror of your heart reflect
when you realize God's plans are
not meant to harm you?

_____

_____

_____

_____

_____

_____

OPEN MY
HEART

*Give me your heart, my son,
and let your eyes delight in my ways.*
PROVERBS 23:26

Open my heart.

Jesus, my friend.

Jesus, my Savior.

Help me comprehend
your love for me.

Help me grasp how wide, long,
high, and deep your love is for me.

I am beautiful for your purpose.

*We are God's handiwork, created in Christ Jesus to do good
works, which God prepared in advance for us to do.*
EPHESIANS 2:10 NIV

Chapter Twenty-Five

AN OPEN HEART

Give me your heart, and let your eyes observe my ways.
PROVERBS 23:26 NKJV

FROM THE BEAUTY KIT

The word *open* describes a situation where we are unguarded or emotionally approachable, where a door is unfastened or unlocked, or the act of starting or beginning something such as a new venture.

Imagine that you're getting ready to leave your house for church or that you're about to walk out the door for a big date. You look in the mirror and notice your hair is sticking straight out on one side or your lipstick has smeared onto your teeth. Do you ignore it and walk out the door? No, you fix it before you leave.

Picture yourself walking through a big mall. You pass by a large plate-glass mirror and realize your shirt is on inside out, then you look down and see that you have on one navy shoe and one black shoe, and you've been out in public like that all day. Your friend has been with you and she didn't say a word. I don't know about you, but I'd smack her on the arm and say, "Why didn't you tell me I looked like this? You're supposed to be my friend!"

Most of us have something inside us that makes us want to fix things when they're messed up. We care about what other people think and we worry that others will believe we look stupid or ugly.

> When our hearts are filled to overflowing with Jesus, he can groom us to do great and mighty things for him.

But sometimes we're not quite so diligent when it comes to our inner beauty. Something the pastor says shines a light on a spot on our heart: a soiled place that needs to be cleaned. But we just brush his words off and go on with what we're doing. We read our Bibles and see things that need to be fixed, and we just ignore them. Or maybe God sends conviction about something he has asked us to quit doing and we pay no attention to that still small voice.

We shut our ears. We ignore the one who loves us most, the one who wants what is best for us. When we do that, we close off our hearts to him. Maybe it's time for us to care more about what Jesus thinks.

He stands there saying, "Let me in. I can fix what's bothering you." But we pay no attention to him. He says, "I can take care of the fears and the pain that are suffocating you." But we don't trust him. He says, "I can forgive your transgressions." But we think we're too bad for him to love us.

It's hard to do much with a closed-off heart, but Jesus, our best friend, says, "I see things you need to change. Open your heart to me, precious child. Let me in and I can fix the flaws. Let me in and I'll erase the painful things of your past. Let me in and I can fill your heart with so much love that you can't contain it. Let me in and I can give you hope and a future."

When our hearts are filled to overflowing with Jesus, he can groom us to do great and mighty things for him.

Dear Jesus, there have been times when I've closed my heart to you. I've shut you out because I wanted my own way because of my fears or because I didn't want to do what you asked me to do. I've discovered I don't like the way that makes me feel. Open my heart, Lord. Give me the faith and courage to trust again. Let me see your glory with fresh eyes. Let me feel your peace, joy, and grace. Fill my heart to overflowing so I can be beautiful for you. Open my heart to others so I respond to them with your love and mercy. Amen.

BEAUTY QUESTIONNAIRE

1. Why do you sometimes close your heart to God?
2. Why does he want you to open your heart to him?
3. How does it make you feel when you close your heart to God? How do you feel when you open it to him?

GET YOUR STILETTOS MOVING

Set aside some time to pray. Say these words, "God, my heart is open to you. I want to listen to you today. Show me what I need to fix in my life. Show me what you want me to do. Show me how I can draw closer to you." Sit and make a list as God speaks to your heart.

THE MIRROR OF YOUR HEART

What does the mirror of your heart reflect when you ask God to open your heart?

_____

_____

_____

_____

_____

_____

Chapter Twenty-Six

A BEAUTIFUL FRIEND

*A man who has friends must himself be friendly, but there is
a friend who sticks closer than a brother.*
PROVERBS 18:24 NKJV

FROM THE BEAUTY KIT

The word *friend* describes someone who is close to a person and
for whom there is love and affection. The word *Jesus* describes the
Son of God, the one who sticks closer than a brother,
and the one who loves us so much that he gave his life
on the cross in our place.

I was born without any fashion sense. None. Nada. Zip. Zilch.
So shopping can be a bit stressful as I try on outfit after outfit
without confidence that any of it looks good on me, especially
since I'm (ahem) horizontally-challenged.

That's why I love to take friends shopping with me: extra
opinions are always helpful. I've discovered something along the
way—some friends are better to take shopping than others. I have
friends who will tell me outfits look good because they don't want

to hurt my feelings, and then I get home with clothing that I'll maybe wear once or twice (usually until I see myself wearing it in a picture and realize that it's not the least bit flattering). The item will then hang in my closet until I make a trip to drop things off at a local resale shop.

I like to take one particular friend with me when I go shopping. She has great fashion sense, but more importantly, she is honest with me. She tells me when things don't look good, when they do, and she makes suggestions for accessories. She is honest with me because she loves me and I appreciate that.

> We can trust God with everything because he is a friend who will never let us down.

Besides that, she has been my encourager through the years. She has prayed for and with me, walked through difficult days with me, celebrated good times with me, loved me enough to give me tough love when needed, and been a faithful friend for over fifty years. She has been wonderful, but I have one friend that is even better than her—Jesus.

It boggles my mind that the God of the world wants to be our friend and that he wants to stay close to us. He is our friend. Our Savior. The lover of our soul. He brings us peace during troubled days, forgives us when we don't deserve it, provides what we need, speaks truth to our hearts, keeps us safe, and is with us every moment of every day. He thinks we're beautiful, and we are, because we're made in his image.

With his friendship comes responsibility. This is a two-way relationship. Just as he listens patiently to us, we need to make time to listen to his sweet whispers to our soul. We need to read his Word: his love letter to us. We need to care for others as he has cared for us. We need to love him more than we love ourselves, to surrender our all to him, knowing that placing our lives in his hands is the safest place to be. We can trust God with everything because he is a friend who will never let us down.

Jesus is the most beautiful and special friend we'll ever have. More than anything, I want to be a beautiful, faithful friend to him. Don't you?

Jesus, you are my dearest friend. Help me to grasp how deep your love is for me. You've been my friend through good times and bad, and I can't imagine walking through life without you. Help me to feel your presence closer to me each day. I want to see you in a new way, and I want my life and soul to be divinely beautiful for you. Thank you for always carrying the pain and stresses of my day, for holding my hand and providing comfort whenever I need you. I love you, and I'm so grateful you're my friend. Amen.

BEAUTY QUESTIONNAIRE

1. Why is it important to have a friend who's honest with you? How does that also apply to God?
2. What does it mean to you to have Jesus as your friend?
3. How can you be a good friend to him and how can you allow him to take the lead in your friendship?

GET YOUR STILETTOS MOVING

Think of a friend who has been there for you and send a thank-you note. Make a list of ways that God has been a good friend to you, then thank him for all that he has done, and ask him to make you a more beautiful friend for him each day.

THE MIRROR OF YOUR HEART

JESUS, MY FRIEND.

What does the mirror of your heart reflect about having Jesus as your friend?

_____

_____

_____

_____

_____

_____

_____

Chapter Twenty-Seven

LIMP HAIR

*This is good, and pleases God our Savior, who wants all
people to be saved and to come to a knowledge of the truth.*
1 Timothy 2:3-4 NIV

FROM THE BEAUTY KIT

The word *savior* describes someone who saves people from
dangerous things or life-threatening moments. The capitalized
word *Savior* describes Jesus, who gave his life for ours.

I am sometimes a bit OCD about my hair and makeup. Part
of it is due to insecurity because of things I lived through in my
childhood. And part of it is because I'm scary-looking until I
put my face on and tame my hair. Just ask my young grandson
who spent the night with us. When we got up the next morning,
he took one look at me and said, "Grandmama, your hair looks
crazy—like a wild animal." Oh, the honesty of children!

Now that you know these important facts about me, you'll
understand why I was a bit upset about something that happened
while I was away for a speaking engagement. I'd shampooed my

hair the morning I left. Since I'd just be there overnight, I figured I wouldn't need to wash it again the next morning, so I left my blow dryer at home. I was staying with my dear friends, Carl and Donnalynn and figured I could use hers if I needed one.

All was going well the next morning until I accidentally soaked my hair in the shower. I got dressed and went to ask Donnalynn if I could borrow her blow dryer.

Then my panic moment arrived. She said, "I don't have one. I air-dry my hair." *My* hair is baby fine, and if I don't dry it, it's limp as can be. Carl graciously offered his Shop Vac to blow my hair, but I suspected that would cause even more problems.

I dried it as best I could with my fingers, and then I heard God whisper to my soul, "It's not about you today, it's about me." *Whew.* I'd been worried about my audience's eyes being on me, when I needed to be more worried about them being on Jesus.

I heard God whisper to my soul: "It's not about you today, it's about me."

I went to speak that day with limp hair and a desire for them to see Jesus as I spoke about how He'd saved me from the pits of hell, how he wants to be our Savior, how He'd been there to offer comfort whenever I needed it, his loving presence wrapping around me like a hug from heaven.

I shared about the painful moments of my childhood, and how their ministry would help children wounded by circumstances and by those who should have been loving and kind to them.

Jesus wants us to give him the memories that haunt us, the words that ring true but are false, the lies that are swarming in our brains. He wants to be the Savior of broken relationships, to take away our negativity, and to teach us about forgiveness. He desires to give us an unexplainable peace for every situation we face. Then when he has brought us out on the other side from our difficult circumstances, he wants us to tell others about him even if we have to stand in front of a crowd and do it with limp hair.

Dear Jesus, I worry so much about looking beautiful (or not beautiful) in my outward appearance. Yet I rarely think about wanting others to see a beautiful spirit in me that will help them to see you. God, open my heart to you. I want to listen to you today. Remind me that it's not about me. It truly is all about you. Thank you for being my Savior, my best friend, and my provider. Make yourself real to me today so I'll walk with you as you guide each step that I take. Make me a bright and shining light for you, a woman of divine beauty whose life will be a daily witness of a precious Savior and his amazing love. Amen.

BEAUTY QUESTIONNAIRE

1. Do you sometimes focus on yourself more than you focus on Jesus?
2. How can moments from your past sometimes derail you as you seek to tell others about Jesus?
3. What has your Savior done for you?

GET YOUR STILETTOS MOVING

There's no greater gift than a Savior who loves you so much he gave his life for you. Think of two people who need to hear about Jesus. Pray for them first, and then reach out and tell them the most beautiful news ever.

THE MIRROR OF YOUR HEART

What does the mirror of your heart reflect
about having Jesus as your Savior?

_____

_____

_____

_____

_____

_____

_____

Chapter Twenty-Eight

NO LIMITS

That Christ may dwell in your hearts through faith; and
that you, being rooted and grounded in love, may be able to
comprehend with all the saints what is the breadth and length
and height and depth, and to know the love of Christ.

Ephesians 3:17-19

FROM THE BEAUTY KIT

The word *grasp* means to grab hold or to have an understanding
of something. The word *wide* refers to something that is extensive.
The word *long* describes something lengthy. The word *high*
describes something of extraordinary height. The word *deep* refers
to something that is bottomless.

The two photos on my computer screen were startling. The
first picture was of a young woman with wavy hair and a cute
figure. Her skin was clear and glowing. She had that healthy girl-
next-door prettiness that you'd notice in a crowd, and her zest for
life radiated from the picture.

The second photo of the woman was about ten years later, and it made my jaw drop. She looked forty years older. Her once-lovely hair was limp. The woman's leathery skin was pale and marked with sores, and her eyes were jaded. Her slumped shoulders gave testimony to her defeated spirit, and her figure was so emaciated that it looked like skin had been stretched across her bones. Meth and other drugs had taken a heavy toll, and they'd taken her far from the faith that had once been part of her life.

> God's love is so wide, long, high, and deep that we can't grasp it, but no matter what we do, we can never out-run it.

Many people would look at her and write her off as a hopeless loser, but Jesus looked at her through his rose-colored glasses of grace and said, "I still love you, my daughter. I know what you once were. I see what you are now. I know that my love and mercy are enough to draw you away from the drugs and back to me. There is *nothing* that you can do that will make me stop loving you."

God's love is so wide, long, high, and deep that we can't grasp it, but no matter what we do, we can never out-run it. It's a love so profound that he sent his only Son to face a brutal death on the cross for us. Jesus did it willingly, and *you* were on his mind.

We might not have messed up our lives with drugs, but all of us have sinned and done wrong. All of us have grieved the heart of God. When we come to him and say, "I'm sorry, and I want you to be my Savior and Lord," he is waiting for us with outstretched arms.

Friend, do you need to do that today?

It's impossible to wrap our finite minds around the complexity of God's love, but we can be secure in it. We don't have to worry that he'll ever stop loving us. Romans 8:38-39 tells us, "I am convinced that neither death nor life, nor angels, nor principalities, nor things present, nor things to come, nor powers, nor height, nor depth, nor any other created thing, will be able to separate us from the love of God, which is in Christ Jesus our Lord."

Receiving God's love and forgiveness isn't where the story ends for us. Once we've encountered that love, we have a responsibility to tell others about it. Our world so desperately needs God's love. What could be more beautiful than a woman who reaches out to others to share the fantastic news that there's a God who loves them?

Dear Father, help me to truly grasp how wide, high, long, and deep your love is for me. I have trouble wrapping my mind around something so amazing. I'm so grateful that you're a God who changes lives. Thank you for changing mine. Thank you for your grace and forgiveness. Father, sometimes I'm my own worst critic. I look at myself and wonder how you could possibly love someone as messed up as me, but you do. Help me to look at others through your eyes, and help me to share the beautiful message of your love. Amen.

BEAUTY QUESTIONNAIRE

1. Why do you need God's love, mercy, and forgiveness?
2. How can God's love change you?
3. What is God's response when you come to him and ask forgiveness?

GET YOUR STILETTOS MOVING

Stop and truly think about the four words: wide, high, long, and deep. Search your heart for how these words provide security about God's love for you, then ask God to place three people on your heart (or in your path) who need to hear about his limitless love.

THE MIRROR OF YOUR HEART

HELP ME GRASP
HOW WIDE, LONG,
HIGH, AND DEEP
GOD'S LOVE
IS FOR ME.

How does it affect the mirror of your heart when you truly understand the limitless depth of God's love for you?

_____

_____

_____

_____

_____

_____

_____

Chapter Twenty-Nine

A GOD WHO LOVES

We have known and believed the love that God has for us.
God is love, and he who abides in love abides in God,
and God in him.
I JOHN 4:16 NKJV

FROM THE BEAUTY KIT

The word *love* describes the emotion of having deep feelings for someone or something. The word *master* denotes someone who is exceptionally skilled at a task.

Have you ever had a professional do your makeup or hair? I had a friend who was an artist when it came to that. I needed some new author photos, and by the time my friend finished my makeup and my hair, I looked so much better than my normal me that I was afraid people wouldn't recognize me when I went to teach at conferences. Either that, or they'd think, *Wow, she has really gone downhill since she had those photos taken.*

Jenn did a modeling campaign in China awhile back, and makeup artist extraordinaire Bro. Chen did some stunning work on her. I remember seeing some of her portfolio photos, and I didn't even recognize that they were Jenn until I looked at them a second time. He was able to alter her appearance that much with just makeup and hair.

A while back, one of our upscale department stores brought in a specialist who was a master when it came to makeup. I signed up for an appointment because I always get great tips from those sessions. I felt like a queen after he worked his magic on me. For the rest of the day, I received tons of comments. "You look so pretty today." Or "Wow, your eyes pop. I've never noticed how beautiful they were before today."

There's just something about the touch of a master's hand.

We've talked a lot about *our* beauty in this book, but today, let's think about *God's* beauty. Imagine that Jesus is sitting next to you as if you were having coffee with a dear friend. See him as real. He is radiant, beautiful. See his holiness and his goodness. See his love.

> We are beautiful not because of who we are but because of the touch of the Master's hand in our lives.

It's life-changing when we truly realize the depth of God's love for us, when we come to understand that he delights in us. Did you comprehend that, sweet friend? The God who made us *delights* in us, and he loves us.

Have you ever seen a young woman who's just become engaged or a bride on her wedding day? Their faces are radiant because they know they are loved. God's love is even better than that. It's eternal. This love gives us an intimate connection to Jesus. He is our companion, our best friend who will never leave or forsake us. He is a lamp to our footsteps, guiding us each day.

Jenn and I both felt prettier because of the skills of the

makeup artists, but those skills were nothing in comparison to the God who designed us, who made us in his image. We are beautiful not because of who we are or what we do, but because of the touch of the Master's hand in our lives and his deep love for us. When we hold his hand tightly and stay close to him, our beauty reflects a God who is so beautiful, awesome, and loving that there are no words to describe it.

Dear Father, it blows me away that the God who made the universe loves me. Help me to return that love to you. Help me to spend time with you, to see you with fresh eyes. I'm so grateful for your unconditional love, Father. Sometimes I fret because I'm not "this" or "that" when it comes to beauty. Remind me that you knit me together in my mother's womb, that I was designed by the Master's hand exactly how you wanted me to be. Help me to hold tightly to your hand, to stay so close to you that I become more like you each day. I want to be a beautiful reflection of a God who is beyond beautiful. Amen.

BEAUTY QUESTIONNAIRE

1. God says he knit you together in your mother's womb. What does that mean to you?
2. How does the touch of the Master's hand make a difference?
3. What do you think is beautiful about God?

GET YOUR STILETTOS MOVING

God's love is amazing, but sometimes we get used to it and we don't stop to think about how blessed we are to have it. Sit down today and think through your life. Make a list of the ways that God has shown his love to you. Then go out and show his love to others.

THE MIRROR OF YOUR HEART

HELP ME COMPREHEND YOUR LOVE FOR ME.

How does it affect the mirror of your heart when you truly get the scope of God's love for you?

_____

_____

_____

_____

_____

_____

_____

Chapter Thirty

SUCH A TIME

*"If you remain completely silent at this time, relief and
deliverance will arise for the Jews from another place, but you
and your father's house will perish. Yet who knows whether
you have come to the kingdom for such a time as this?"*

ESTHER 4:14 NKJV

FROM THE BEAUTY KIT

The word *purpose* describes the act of becoming what you were
created for or something you intend to do. The word *divine*
describes us as becoming like God.

Talk about a beauty pageant! The king's representatives had
searched the kingdom for the most beautiful women they could
find as possibilities for the next queen. All of them were brought
to the palace.

Esther was a Jewish orphan, but in that sea of beautiful
women, there was something about her that made her stand out.
There was an inner beauty and the favor of God. The king loved
her best and made her the new queen.

But that was just part of God's plan for Esther. He had a bigger
purpose for her. When wicked Haman set out to destroy the Jews,

her uncle, Mordecai, sent word for Esther to go before the king and request mercy for her people. Visiting the king without an invitation meant she might be put to death, but Mordecai told her, "Who knows whether you have come to the kingdom for such a time as this?"

The Jews fasted for her, and then she stepped out in faith for the purpose that God had designed just for her. Because of her faithfulness, her people were spared, and this beautiful woman left behind a story to inspire all of us.

To become a woman of true beauty like Esther, we must fill our lives with God's truths and take on his attributes of purity, holiness, mercy, wisdom, compassion, courage, and faithfulness. We must groom our hearts daily, cleansing away the imperfections, applying his Word to every aspect, and fashioning our lives after him.

> Each of us will face that "for such a time as this" moment in our lives, that time when we will, or we won't, do what God has asked us to do.

There is only so much we can accomplish with our outward beauty, and time will take a toll on that. But with our inner beauty, there's no limit. We have the ability to become more beautiful until the end of our lives. There's a reason for that inner beauty: to please the heart of God, to reach others for him, and to achieve the purposes he designed for us before we were even born.

Each of us will face that "for such a time as this" moment in our lives, that time when we will, or we won't, do what God has asked us to do.

It would be a shame to stand before God someday and hear him say, "You wasted the opportunities that I gave you. I had a purpose for your life, but you missed it. I wanted to be close to you, I wanted you to become beautiful for me, but you had other things to do that you thought were more important."

Sweet friend, today is the day to determine that you *will* become the woman of divine beauty that God desires, that you'll fulfill the purpose he has for you, and that you'll live so close to him that you can almost feel the warmth of his hand on your shoulder.

Each day as you go out on the catwalk of life, model Jesus for everyone, knowing that he has made *you* divinely beautiful so others can see him through you.

Dear Father, I realize that you have a purpose for my life. Please don't let me leave that purpose unfulfilled. Take away the lies I've believed about myself and the words that others have spoken to me. Instead of looking at my inabilities, help me to see your abilities that are without limits. Instead of focusing on my failures, help me to look ahead to what you can make of me if I apply your truths to my life, and if I fashion myself after your attributes. Lord, make me a woman of great beauty not for my glory, but for yours. Give me an inner beauty that comes from a heart that is chasing after you. Help my life to please you. Amen.

BEAUTY QUESTIONNAIRE

1. In a sea of beauty, what made Esther stand out? What can make *you* stand out from the crowd?
2. What can keep you from fulfilling the purpose that God has for you?
3. How can you prepare for that "such a time as this" moment in your life?

GET YOUR STILETTOS MOVING

Make a two-column list. In the first column, list the things you can learn from the life of Esther. In the second column, list what you'd like to change about your life spiritually so that you can live a life of courage and faithfulness like Esther did.

THE MIRROR OF YOUR HEART

BEAUTIFUL FOR
HIS PURPOSE.

How does it affect the mirror of your heart when you realize that God has made you beautiful for *his* purpose?

_____

_____

_____

_____

_____

_____

THE WOMAN IN MY MIRROR

MICHELLE COX

I look in the mirror,
and what do I see?
A far-from-perfect woman
looking back at me.
She's having a bad hair day,
a red bump is on her pug nose,
and, oh to my soul!
Is that chipped polish on her toes?
What about those wrinkles,
crow's feet, and old age spots
that had the nerve to show up
despite cold creams that were bought.
Is that dress a Goodwill reject?
Where'd she get those shoes?
Forget a beauty pageant,
it's a cinch she would lose.
Oh my, the figure!
Enormous hips and thunder thighs.
If they gave a trophy for "Biggest
    Gainer"
she'd surely win the prize.
A makeover is in order,
a pedicure and a day at the spa,
then a facial and a shopping trip
for Spanx and a Wonder Bra.
All of it's in vain
because no matter what I try,

that less-than-perfect woman
is still what meets my eye.
Yes, I'm the woman in the mirror.
I spend my time on the outward me,
When what's really more important
is what does Jesus see?
When he looks in the mirror of my life
and how I've spent each day,
I hope I've not disappointed him,
but I'm afraid to hear what he'd say.
That mirror of my life might change
if each day were a spa for the soul,
spent pampering my prayer life,
pleasing God as my ultimate goal.
Exfoliating my soul's flaws,
tweezing faults that must go away,
becoming fashioned in his likeness,
and spending time with him each day.
So, Lord, whenever you look at me,
I hope that what you see
is a woman who longs to be like you
because then a true beauty I'll be.
When others see the mirror of my life,
there's one thing I hope they can do:
when they look at that shiny reflection,
all they can see is you.

ACKNOWLEDGMENTS

A book like this doesn't just happen, and we are so thankful for everyone who helped us make *Divine Beauty* a reality.

Thank you to Joel Bunkoswke and Jim E. Chandler, co-creators of The Farmer and The Belle, for all your support and help, and most of all, your prayers. We couldn't have done this without you.

Many thanks to Michelle Winger at Literally Precise for your editorial talents and the creative designs by Chris Garborg for crafting a beautiful book.

Thank you to Erin Smalley, Arolyn Burns, Sue Silvestri, and Jacqui Phillips for providing additional insights to us women for a pathway to biblical beauty.

We couldn't do what we do without our prayer team and we are so grateful for their faithfulness in praying for us and for our work.

Our agent, Tamela Hancock Murray is a gift. She is always such an encouragement and blessing. Tamela, thank you for your wisdom and for your prayers.

Both of us are blessed with the best husbands ever. Thank you to Paul Cox and Jim Chandler for their love, for always being so encouraging, and for their prayers as we worked on this project.

Most of all, we're so grateful to God for this opportunity. Our prayer for this book was that God would send us the words that he wanted on the pages. All glory and honor go to him.

We are so excited to share this devotional book about divine beauty with you. Sweet friends, we have prayed for you as we've worked on this book, and we hope that through the pages of *Divine Beauty,* you'll discover that nothing is more beautiful than a woman who is sold out to God. *You* can be that woman.

With love,

Michelle and Jean

ABOUT THE AUTHORS

Known for her "encouragement with a Southern drawl," **Michelle Cox** is a speaker and an award-winning, best-selling author. She's the co-author of the *When God Calls the Heart* devotional book series based on Hallmark's #1 show, *When Calls the Heart.*

Michelle has written for *Guideposts,* Focus on the Family, FoxNews.com, Christian Cinema, *WHOA Magazine for Women, Leading Hearts Magazine,* and the website of Fox News Radio Host Todd Starnes. She is the creator of the Just 18 Summers® brand of parenting products and resources, and has been a guest on numerous television and radio programs, including *Home & Family, Hannity,* and *Focus on the Family.*

She and her husband, Paul, have been married for 44 years, and have three sons, three lovely daughters-in-law, and seven perfect grandchildren. Connect with Michelle at WhenGodCallstheHeart.com, www.just18summers.com, on Twitter @MichelleInspire, and on Facebook at www.Facebook.com/MichelleCoxInspirations.

Jenn Gotzon's career break came from playing President Nixon's daughter, Tricia, in the five-time Oscar-nominated film *Frost/Nixon.* This launched Jenn into family movies on Amazon, and brought about awards for *Doonby, God's Country,* and *Saving Faith.* With two Academy Award-nominated films under her belt, Jenn has developed a niche playing real-life characters in values-based cinema, for example, *My Daddy's in Heaven.* Ted Baehr with MovieGuide, states, "Jenn Gotzon reveals character with an extraordinary emotional range, better than almost anyone in Hollywood today!"

Jenn is passionate about impacting and inspiring audiences as a public speaker, and through the movies she appears in alongside her husband, Jim E. Chandler. *The Farmer and The Belle* (movies, books and jewelry) is her ministry, providing a pathway to true beauty and real love, for girls of all ages to have a healthy identity that's based in godly values. She tours globally sharing her mission in Asia, Europe, and throughout America. Jenn loves worshipping God, watching sunsets with her love, and playing games with her family. Follow @JennGotzon on Instagram and text the word INSPIRING to 22828 to receive a fun movie gift and read her newsletter.

PSYCHOLOGY APPROACH TO DIVINE BEAUTY

Erin Smalley, BSN, MS, LPCC

We *all* have lies written on our hearts. We can't see them, yet they affect how we see ourselves and interact with the world. Maybe like Belle from *The Farmer and the Belle* movie, it's because you think something is wrong with you or your body—in essence "I'm ugly, fat, and unworthy." Though others try to tell you this isn't true, you don't believe them.

But you can govern your thoughts with truth.

Let the words of my mouth, and the meditation of my heart, be acceptable in thy sight, O Lord, my strength, and my redeemer. Psalm 19:14 KJV

Make sure your self-talk is gracious and kind. Don't speak to yourself in a way you wouldn't speak to someone you love. Your heavenly Father wants you to stop putting yourself down.

Proverbs 18:21 (NIV) says, "The tongue has the power of life and death."

Identify the negative voices in your life and surround yourself with people who speak positively to you.

You don't have to do it by yourself. As a believer, you have the spirit of truth in you to lead you toward healing and truth. It's worth the battle to seek healing around these lies. It will impact how you show up in every situation.

"When he, the Spirit of truth, comes, he will guide you into all the truth." John 16:13 NIV

"You shall know the truth, and the truth shall make you free." John 8:32 NKJV

*Discover more about Erin on Focus on the Family and in her book, *The Wholehearted Wife: 10 Keys to a More Loving Relationship.*

NUTRITION TIPS TO DIVINE BEAUTY

Susan Silvestri

Your body is the outward representation of the inward you. When your body is operating at its full potential, you are more apt to have a healthy mindset and vibrant spirit. Nutrition and exercise help to keep your body fit. This, in turn, frees you to do physical activities. Sometimes you need to remove the pressure to be perfect, allowing God to give you the discipline and joy to help in this process.

You were created to use your body for more than just outward appearance. Your body functions as an instrument to not only accomplish tasks, but to be a display of splendor, an expression of praise and glory. (Excerpted from page 71.)

Nutrition and exercise are not a diet and fitness program but a lifestyle. The key is balance and grace. Eating fit foods (nutritional) can alter your life and create habits of health and wellness. Allowing yourself the occasional free food (like dark chocolate) gives variety and keeps you out of bondage. Staying away from fake food (processed, refined food) can keep you from the stuff that is harmful to you.

Exercise to stay fit but allow yourself the joy and freedom within that.

It is this balance of discipline and grace
While you are running your life's race
With the vision to be the best *you* can be
That will keep you wHoly fit and wHoly free!
(Excerpted from page 212.)

Learn more about Susan at SusanSilvestri.com or her book *wHoly Fit, wHoly Free* at Amazon.com.

THERAPY STEPS TO DIVINE BEAUTY

Arolyn Burns, LPCC, LMFT, Coach, Author
and Inspirational Speaker

Growing up, I was bullied. I felt ugly, unloved, and like a complete outcast. In high school, even though I made the #1 drill team in the nation, I didn't feel like I was good enough.

I am grateful for those experiences as they taught me to lean on Christ, to have compassion for others, and to reach out to the outcast or unlovable. Our true worth is innate. We are created "in the image of God." He knit us together in our mother's womb. I tell all my clients "You are perfectly you." We have all heard that God doesn't make mistakes. And what's really cool is that he planned *you*. You have strengths and talents and were created for a purpose. Thrive in who you were created to be.

If everyone were the same, we would be cookie-cutter Stepford wives. How boring. Be you. Be free. Know the One who created the universe created you in all your silly, crazy, creative, fun, interesting, loveable uniqueness.

The Bible says to hold every thought captive:

1. Each time you notice a negative thought—say out loud, "That's not true."

2. Say a positive alternative out loud (the stronger and more truthful the better).

3. Redirect your thoughts to the present moment. Be mindful of what is in front of you, for example, a sunset or the details of flowers.

Visit Arolyn Burns at TheATreatment.com.

COSMETIC TIPS TO DIVINE BEAUTY

JACQUI PHILLIPS

Beauty is in your heart and soul, not in the eyes of the beholder, and words are powerful.

Words can attach themselves to your inner mind and affect the way you feel about yourself.

God made us all unique, so why not love what makes you, *you*!

Perception matters. Embrace your beauty, and here's how:

For the face, prep, prime, primp. Start with clean skin, toner if needed. For best results, use a moisturizer, primer, concealer, and foundation. Don't forget to blend—it is truly your best friend. To look like a pro, forgetting your neck is a no-go.

Your eyebrows are often unsung heroes, they frame the face, opening up your eyes, and even can give you an eye-lift. Don't underestimate the power of your brows. Make your brows work for you.

For next level allure, contouring and highlighting is what you're looking for.

Eye makeup is a personal experience. Period. Make sure to choose a color palette that complements your skin tone. Again, *blend*. Don't forget to have fun with this as this feature is a great opportunity to let your personality shine.

As women, we influence, empower, and nurture many people. With that being said, please remember to go out in the world with love, and offer the world your best you.

Believe Love of Ourselves Matters—B-L-O-O-M into beautiful.

*Jacqui Phillips is a celebrity makeup artist, best-selling, and award-winning author of *Reset: 6 Essential Resets to a Healthier Happier You*. www.jacquiphillips.tv @jacquijphillips

Special thanks to Arolyn Burns, LPCC, for her friendship and prayers and for her generous sponsorship to make *Divine Beauty* become a reality.

Have you ever had a bad day and needed someone to listen, help you process things, or talk you off a ledge? At the "A" Treatment Center, they don't just heal, they transform. Arolyn specializes in anxiety, phobias, trauma, and chronic pain. For more information, visit her website at TheATreatment.com.

#Beauty Bracelet™ is a beautiful chain that holds five charms which affirm the mind, body, and soul on what true beauty and real love divinely are.